AFRICAN ETHNOGRAPHIC STUDIES
OF THE 20TH CENTURY

Volume 35

WITCHCRAFT, SORCERY AND SOCIAL CATEGORIES AMONG THE SAFWA

WITCHCRAFT, SORCERY AND SOCIAL CATEGORIES AMONG THE SAFWA

ALAN HARWOOD

LONDON AND NEW YORK

First published in 1970 by Oxford University Press for the International African Institute.

This edition first published in 2018
by Routledge
2 Park Square, Milton Park, Abingdon, Oxon OX14 4RN

and by Routledge
711 Third Avenue, New York, NY 10017

Routledge is an imprint of the Taylor & Francis Group, an informa business

© 1970 International African Institute

All rights reserved. No part of this book may be reprinted or reproduced or utilised in any form or by any electronic, mechanical, or other means, now known or hereafter invented, including photocopying and recording, or in any information storage or retrieval system, without permission in writing from the publishers.

Trademark notice: Product or corporate names may be trademarks or registered trademarks, and are used only for identification and explanation without intent to infringe.

British Library Cataloguing in Publication Data
A catalogue record for this book is available from the British Library

ISBN: 978-0-8153-8713-8 (Set)
ISBN: 978-0-429-48813-9 (Set) (ebk)
ISBN: 978-1-138-59414-2 (Volume 35) (hbk)
ISBN: 978-0-429-48901-3 (Volume 35) (ebk)

Publisher's Note
The publisher has gone to great lengths to ensure the quality of this reprint but points out that some imperfections in the original copies may be apparent.

Disclaimer
The publisher has made every effort to trace copyright holders and would welcome correspondence from those they have been unable to trace.

Headman cutting a special sheaf of millet which is reserved as seed for the following year

WITCHCRAFT, SORCERY, AND SOCIAL CATEGORIES AMONG THE SAFWA

ALAN HARWOOD

Published for the
International African Institute
by the
Oxford University Press
1970

Oxford University Press, Ely House, London W.1

GLASGOW NEW YORK TORONTO MELBOURNE WELLINGTON
CAPE TOWN SALISBURY IBADAN NAIROBI LUSAKA ADDIS ABABA
BOMBAY CALCUTTA MADRAS KARACHI LAHORE DACCA
KUALA LUMPUR SINGAPORE HONG KONG TOKYO

© International African Institute 1970

*Printed in Great Britain
by Ebenezer Baylis and Son, Ltd.
The Trinity Press, Worcester, and London*

TABLE OF CONTENTS

Preface ix
A note on Safwa orthography xiii
Introduction xv

I. AN INTRODUCTION TO MWANABANTU AREA 1
    The environment
    Subsistence
    Social structure

II. DISEASE, DEATH, DEVIANCE, AND THE ANCESTORS 30
    The concept of *empongo*
    The general causes of *empongo* as revealed in ancestor rites
    Summary and conclusions

III. SAFWA AETIOLOGICAL CATEGORIES 48
    Divination and autopsy: the background
    The causes of *empongo*
    Itonga and witchcraft, medicines and sorcery: a comparative view of Safwa beliefs

IV. AETIOLOGICAL CATEGORIES AND THE DIAGNOSIS OF *EMPONGO* 77
    Nature of the data
    Case studies in the causation of *empongo*
    Summary and conclusions

V. A PRAGMATIC ANALYSIS OF THE AETIOLOGY OF *EMPONGO* 110
    Nature of the evidence
    The uses and effects of formal diagnoses in terms of *itonga*
    The uses and effects of formal diagnoses in terms of medicines
    Summary and conclusions

VI. CONCLUSION 135

    The place of beliefs about *itonga* and medicines in the social life of Mwanabantu tribe

    Relevance of observations among the Mwanabantu to Middleton and Winter's question

Appendix	141
Glossary	151
Bibliography	153
Index	157

LIST OF PLATES

Headman cutting a special sheaf of millet which is reserved as seed for the following year *frontispiece*

facing page

Ia Community in the foothills of the Mbeya range, showing dispersed settlement pattern   30

b Grave of a child who died within the previous month of *empongo embibi*   30

IIa *Empeta*, dance performed at the ceremony for welcoming a dead person to the White Place, the land of the ancestors   31

b Arriving at an ancestor ceremony. The man and woman (*centre*) are bringing supplies for the ceremony while the others dance out to greet them   31

IIIa Paraphernalia ready for an ancestor ceremony: pots and gourds of beer, white cocks, trays of millet flour, and a butchered calf (*rear*). The grave is marked by the tree trunk (*centre*)   46

b Food distribution at ancestor rites. An officiant is cutting pieces of meat for distribution to key kinsmen of the deceased. This is done before the prayers are begun   46

IVa The *eshiponyo*. The officiant pours beer into one of the two holes which have been dug for the dead. Millet flour and meat have already been placed around the holes   47

b Cock being offered to the ancestors. The head of the fowl is being held in the beer which has been poured for the ancestors   47

LIST OF TABLES

		page
I	Frequency of divinations and their immediate causes	51
II	Clients seeking initial divinations for various precipitating situations	52
III	Summary of interpretations of Mwalyego's death	82
IV	Summary of interpretations concerning the death of Mpɛnza's son	87
V	Summary of cases highlighting relevant variables	100–101
VI	Divined causes of *empongo* and barrenness; proportions of various diagnoses from diviner's records and anecdotal reports	112

LIST OF FIGURES

1. Diagram of the ground plan of a compound	11
2. Mwanabantu and Mabande tribal genealogies and the geographical location of tribal segments	21
3. Reputed genealogical relationship of individuals mentioned in quotations from Ceremony 2	39
4. Taxonomy of *onzizi*	63

LIST OF MAPS

1. Peoples of the Tanganyika-Nyasa Corridor (after Wilson, 1958)	3
2. Tribes of the Safwa dialect area	4

PREFACE

I came to write about witchcraft and sorcery among the Safwa by a very indirect route. In the spring of 1962 I was awarded a Pre-Doctoral Research Training Fellowship from the Social Science Research Council (U.S.) to prepare a general ethnography of the Kinga, a group located in the Livingstone Mountains of what was then the Southern Highlands Region of Tanganyika. I had selected the Kinga partly because of their scanty coverage in the ethnographic literature but mainly because I was interested in problems of swidden agriculture in a mountain environment.

About six weeks before leaving for East Africa, I learned that another anthropologist, Dr. George Park, had already begun research among the Kinga. On arrival, I met with Park and Dr. Derek Stenning, who was then Chairman of the East African Institute of Social Research. For a number of reasons, methodological and financial, we agreed that it was not advisable for two anthropologists to locate among the Kinga. This decision led me to reconnoitre neighbouring peoples. I surveyed the Pangwa, Safwa, and very briefly the Sangu. Since Safwa territory contains mountains, plains, extinct volcanic craters, and other ecological niches which augured well for a study of agricultural techniques, I chose to settle with this group.

Although I gathered material on Safwa agricultural practices (some of which I have reported briefly elsewhere, Harwood 1964), the Safwa themselves led me to another fascinating area of their culture—ideas about the cause of disease and the relationship between these ideas and interpersonal disputes. In this roundabout way I came to write the dissertation on witchcraft, sorcery, and social classification which forms the basis of this book.

Altogether I spent seventeen months among the Safwa from early November 1962, to late March 1964. Approximately fifteen months of this time were spent in one community, which I call Ipepete, and it is largely the kindness and generosity of the people of this settlement which made my field work possible. Since this book often discusses family and other disputes which many of my former neighbours would not want publicized, I have protected their identities by changing all personal names and the names of all communities.

Ipepete, like all Safwa communities, is a group of dispersed compounds and houses. I lived in one of a unique cluster of recently built, rectangular, mudbrick houses, the rest of which were inhabited by young Safwa men and their wives. One of these young men, the son of the local headman, served as my first assistant and teacher of the Safwa language. With his and others' help, I eventually attained sufficient command of the language to be able to conduct my daily activities and question people without the help of an interpreter. I nevertheless went to important interviews or events with an English-speaking assistant who could provide clarification if needed. I did not attain sufficient mastery of Safwa to comprehend fully conversations in which I was not directly involved.

In the early days of my field stay I spent much of my time with young men about 15 to 30 years of age. They and children proved the most patient language teachers. The youths who sought me out tended to be those who had spent some time among strangers at mines either in South Africa or Zambia. Because they were familiar with some features of my world—radios, movies, magazines, African geography—as well as the indigenous world of ancestors, kin responsibilities, and hoe farming, they helped me in the transition to this latter world. In time I talked more and more with the older adults (the 40 to 60 year olds) who were committed to this world, and it was largely they who furthered my understanding of witchcraft and sorcery. To them, thank you—*endaga, mwasalipa*.

I would like to thank the Social Science Research Council (U.S.), which supported my field research, and the U.S. Public Health Service, which awarded me a grant while I was writing up the material. I am also indebted to Professor Harold Conklin for his influence and encouragement during my anthropological training.

In preparing this study for publication, I am particularly grateful for the helpful comments of Professors Morton Fried, Terence Hopkins, John Middleton, and Aidan Southall, all of whom read the manuscript at one or another stage of completion. To them I owe many improvements. I would also like to thank Dr. David Crabb for advising me on Safwa orthography and Mr. Donald Miller for preparing the maps and diagrams. I am indebted to the International

African Institute for undertaking the publication and to Miss Barbara Pym for her editorial assistance.

Lastly, I would like to thank my parents for providing the foundations for my intellectual development and my wife for her patience and invaluable assistance in preparing this manuscript.

A NOTE ON SAFWA ORTHOGRAPHY

The orthography used in this book is based on an analysis of Safwa phonology carried out by the author. Dr. David Crabb kindly lent his assistance in selecting symbols to represent the vowels, but I must take full responsibility for any inadequacies in the analysis.

The symbols used correspond to those recommended by the International African Institute (*Practical Orthography of African Languages*, Oxford, 1962) with the following exceptions: the unvoiced post-alveolar fricative is rendered as 'sh', and all vowels are somewhat more close than their cardinal-position designations would suggest. The phoneme 'b' is heard as a voiced, bi-labial stop only after a nasal and in all other environments as a fricative. Both length and tone are important in the language, although I have not indicated either in the orthography.

Verbs are indicated by their root forms enclosed by hyphens—e.g. *-tat-*, *-ly-*.

INTRODUCTION

In a recent volume on witchcraft and sorcery in East Africa (Middleton and Winter 1963), the editors raise a number of questions about beliefs in wizardry[1] which, they claim, 'have not as yet been raised in any systematic form, let alone answered' (p. 8). One of these questions concerns the reasons why some societies maintain beliefs in both witchcraft and sorcery.

Witchcraft, as defined by Middleton and Winter (p. 3),[2] is 'a mystical and innate power, which can be used by its possessor to harm other people'. Sorcery, on the other hand, is 'evil magic against others'. In further developing this second concept, the editors note that: 'In Africa the most common belief is that sorcerers use "medicines" to harm those against whom they bear ill will' (p. 3). For the purposes of this study, we shall follow Middleton and Winter in their interpretation of these terms and define 'witchcraft' as a belief which attributes misfortune to innate psychic powers and 'sorcery' as a belief attributing misfortune to maleficent physical substances.[3]

Middleton and Winter reason that since either of these beliefs by itself can logically function as an explanation of misfortune and an aid to action in the face of uncertainty, 'one set of beliefs, either those regarding sorcery or those concerning witchcraft, is redundant' (p. 8). They continue,

> If, however, these two types of ideas were fully substitutable for one another, while we might expect to find them co-existing in an occasional society, we would not expect to find them together in one society after another as is the case in Africa. The only reasonable inference is that they must fit into social systems in different ways (p. 8).

---

[1] We are here adopting Middleton and Winter's use of 'wizardry' as a cover term for both witchcraft and sorcery.

[2] These definitions derive from Evans-Pritchard's pioneering study of the Azande (1937).

[3] Douglas's recent (1967:72–3) comments concur with these criteria for defining the distinction between witchcraft and sorcery.

In this study we attempt to make a start in answering Middleton and Winter's important question as to the reasons why beliefs in both witchcraft and sorcery frequently exist simultaneously in the same society by showing how both these beliefs 'fit into' the social system of one African society of which we have first-hand experience: the Mwanabantu tribe[4] of the Safwa dialect group of south-western Tanzania.

In the course of eighteen-months field work among these people, we observed the importance of both witchcraft and sorcery beliefs as explanations of disease and death and undertook a study of the place of these beliefs in the social life of the Mwanabantu. By describing the different, yet complementary, roles that each of these sets of beliefs plays in processes of social control within the tribe, we show that these beliefs not only 'fit into' the social system in different ways, to use Middleton and Winter's phraseology, but are indeed integral to a scheme of classification which is central to the whole social structure of the tribe.

OUTLINE OF THE ARGUMENT

After providing the background by describing the Mwanabantu environment, mode of subsistence, and social system in Chapter I, we begin the analysis of the role of beliefs about witchcraft and sorcery in social life by considering the most common stimuli for expression of these beliefs, instances of disease and death.[5] In Chapter II, therefore, we examine the general ideas held by speakers of the Safwa dialect about the aetiology of disease and death. Following this, in Chapter III we survey the range of aetiological categories recognized by them, first by discussing autopsy and seances, the natural settings for making statements about the aetiology of disease and death in Mwanabantu society. The diagnoses proffered on these occasions provide a universe of aetiological terms which are a complete contrast set—i.e. 'culturally appropriate responses which are distinctive alternatives in the same

[4] The term 'tribe' is defined in the Safwa context as all those communities whose headmen recognize common patrilineal descent. This usage is taken from Evans-Pritchard (1940), who uses it to describe much the same kind of social unit among the Nuer, although he defines the unit in terms of political rights and obligations rather than lineage (p. 5). He notes, however, that Nuer 'habitually' express tribal obligations 'in a kinship idiom' (p. 143). We have chosen to define the unit as Safwa speakers do, in lineage terms.

[5] We are here using the terms 'disease' and 'death' to gloss the single Safwa term *empongo* which is discussed more fully in Chapter II.

Introduction xvii

kinds of situations' (Frake 1962:78). (See also Sturtevant 1964:108–10 for a discussion of the notion of 'contrast set'.)

Taking these aetiological terms, we attempt to discover the principles which govern the application of one of them, rather than another, to particular instances of disease or death. Given our central problem, however, we concentrate analysis only on those terms of the folk aetiology which correspond most nearly to the analytic categories of witchcraft and sorcery.[6] In Chapter IV we thus investigate how Mwanabantu use these terms in concrete instances of disease and death. We shall find that the cause assigned to a case of disease or death depends on the social relationship between antagonists in a dispute which becomes associated with the particular case of illness or death. More specifically, we shall see that the cause is traced to witchcraft (*itonga* in Safwa terminology) when parties to a dispute have an agnatic (incorporative) relationship to one another and to sorcery (*onzizi*—'medicine') when their relationship is one of non-kinsmen (a transactional relationship).

We next proceed (in Chapter V) to investigate what effect the assignment of a case of disease or death to each of these aetiological categories has on the outcome of the underlying dispute—in short, to see the influence which diagnoses of witchcraft or sorcery have on procedures of social control. By doing this, we seek to clarify the way in which the two sets of beliefs, witchcraft and sorcery, fit into the social system of Mwanabantu tribe. We conclude by returning to Middleton and Winter's initial question of why certain societies maintain beliefs in both witchcraft and sorcery and discuss the contribution which the Mwanabantu ethnographic material makes towards its solution.

---

[6] Sturtevant (1964:108) has called attention to the feasibility of undertaking in this manner a paradigmatic analysis of items which do not exhaust the membership of a contrast set and has instanced several articles which have followed this tactic.

For the distinction between folk and analytic categories, see Bohannan (1957; 1963:10–14).

CHAPTER 1

AN INTRODUCTION TO MWANABANTU AREA

The Safwa are a Bantu-speaking people, numbering around 65,000 (East African Statistical Department 1958), who live in the Southern Highlands Region of Tanzania. Apart from their appearance as an entity in travel books, colonial administration records, tribal maps, and ethnographic literature since the nineteenth century, they constitute neither a cultural nor a sociopolitical unit.

Rather, they are a dialect group of a larger linguistic community which includes the Nyiha, Malila, and Mbwila. Culturally, too, they belong to this larger group of 'Nyiha peoples' (Wilson 1958:28–32), living in the border lands between Tanzania, Zambia, and Malawi.[1] There is also no evidence that the people of the Safwa dialect group ever achieved political unity, even under colonial administration. They appear in the earliest records of this area (Fülleborn 1906; Kootz-Kretschmer 1926–9; Thomson 1881) much as they do today: a number of independent tribes,[2] each organized under a separate chiefly lineage.

In view of this situation, the most fruitful ethnographic approach to this area is to proceed on two levels: (1) on the level of the overall Safwa-Nyiha linguistic and cultural unit, and (2) on the level of the independent sociopolitical sub-units which comprise this larger unity. The material presented in this book is concerned almost entirely with the second level. Thus the sociocultural data reported here

[1] On the basis of her 1955 survey of the Nyasa-Tanganyika corridor peoples, Wilson (1958:41) considered it 'quite likely' that the Nyiha and Safwa formed a 'dialect group'. She further spoke of Safwa 'language and customs' as being closer to those of the Nyiha than to the Nyakyusa. My own recorded samples of several Safwa and Nyiha dialects confirm Wilson's impressions about linguistic affinities. With regard to cultural similarities, the work of Bachmann (1943) and Brock (1963, 1966) verifies the close resemblance between the Nyiha of Mbozi and the Safwa, in contrast to the Nyakyusa-Ngonde, Hehe-Bena-Sangu, and probably also Wilson's 'Mwika people' of this region. In discussing the problem of cultural similarities and differences personally with Mrs. Brock and Dr. Mariam Slater, who studied the Nyiha of Mbozi in 1962–3, we have agreed on the validity of considering the two groups as a cultural unit in contrast to the above named groups.

[2] See Introduction, footnote 4, for the definition of this term in the Safwa context.

were collected within one tribal unit, that associated with the chiefly lineage descended from Mwanabantu.

Within Mwanabantu tribe, the ethnographer resided in a community we shall call Ipepete. The original settlement of one of the major segments of Mwanabantu lineage, Ipepete is a community of 440 people located in the foothills of a range of mountains within walking distance of Itimba, the Regional Headquarters, and Magombe, the former seat of one of the British-appointed chiefs.[3] The sociological and cultural observations made in this community were later checked in other communities of the same tribe to ascertain their currency within it.

Although some effort was also made to confirm both the sociological data and interpretations of the cultural code in other Safwa-speaking tribes, it would be misleading to refer these facts to all Safwa. On the one hand, they may be held by only certain of the tribes traditionally labelled by this term; on the other hand, Brock's (1963, 1966) material suggests that they may be shared in considerable detail by all people within the larger cultural unit called the Nyiha people. In view of these different levels of cultural sharing, we shall therefore note, so far as our data allow, whether the facts we are citing pertain only to the Mwanabantu tribe or apply in general to speakers of the Safwa dialect. Thus the social structure, beliefs, etc., which we specifically label 'Safwa' fall into this second category; when not so labelled, the data should be understood to pertain, so far as we know, only to our smaller unit of study.

Map 1 indicates the approximate boundaries of two major areas about which we are concerned: the Nyiha-Safwa culture area and the Safwa dialect area. Map 2 depicts the various tribal regions of the Safwa dialect area with Mwanabantu tribe and its two major subdivisions shaded.

THE ENVIRONMENT

The territory inhabited by Safwa speakers roughly resembles a trough, with a rolling central plain walled in on its northern and

[3] Although Mwanabantu tribe was located near a governmental centre (population, according to the 1957 census, 8,018), it was notorious among Community Development workers for its 'primitivity'—i.e. failure of its people to form a co-operative, to participate significantly in cash cropping, to join the Tanganyika African National Union, and other outward signs of modernity. For reasons stated in the Preface, the above place-names are fictitious.

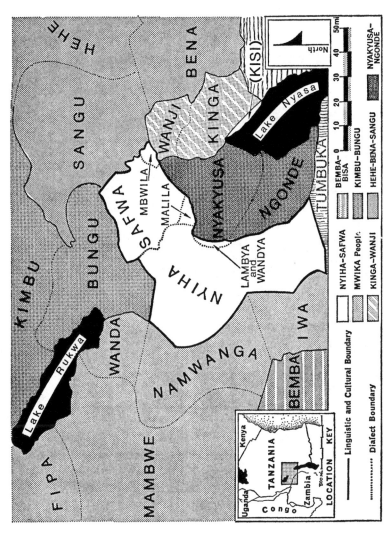

Map 1. Peoples of the Tanganyika–Nyasa Corridor
(after Wilson, 1958)

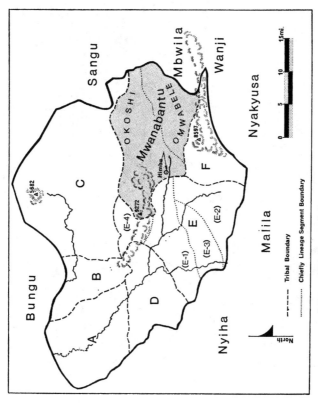

Map 2. Tribes of the Safwa dialect area

southern perimeters by mountain ranges. On its eastern margin the central plain slopes down to the Buhoro Flats—home of the Sangu people, whose cultural and linguistic affinities lie to the north and east. On its western margin the plain rises to the Mbozi Scarp, the eastern border of Nyiha country. To the north-west it tapers slowly to the Lake Rukwa flats and the territory of the Bungu, whose cultural similarities lie with tribes further north.

The central Safwa plain varies in altitude from about 5,000 to 5,700 feet, while the enclosing mountains reach a height of over 9,000 feet. Habitations are located on the central plane and on hills and mountain spurs to an altitude of about 7,500 feet. Above that altitude one finds only occasional huts, inhabited in the rainy season by herdboys.

At lower altitudes the mean annual temperature is about 63° F., with a yearly range of 21 degrees around the mean. As one proceeds up the mountains, however, the average temperature falls about 1 degree for every 300-foot rise in altitude, and frosts occur frequently at around 7,000 feet during the coldest months of June and July.

Like temperature, rainfall in the area also varies directly with altitude. The central plain receives an average of about 35 inches per year, while the mountains receive a mean of 54 inches annually at 6,000 to 7,500 feet and 60 inches or more at higher altitudes (Moffett 1958; McCulloch 1962; East African Meteorological Department, personal communication). Furthermore, over 90% of this rain falls between November and April, with the months of June through August typically rainless. Cloudy and misty conditions are common throughout the higher regions during the entire rainy season, a situation epitomized by the Safwa quip that not even the chickens know when it's morning during the rainy season.

SUBSISTENCE

Agriculture
The Safwa-speaking people are swidden cultivators with a primary dependence on eleusine, sorghum, maize, sweet potatoes, and beans. Secondary crops consist of gourds, tomatoes, a minor root crop (*Coleus esculentus*) and pigeon, cow, and green peas. There are also some regional crop specializations, with manioc and taro grown in certain hotter and dryer lowland areas and white potatoes in the

upper mountains. Agricultural production is primarily the responsibility of women. Each married, able-bodied Safwa woman hoes[4] approximately thirteen garden plots per year, totalling 2·5 to 4 acres. The work of preparing these plots and of weeding and harvesting millet is done in co-operative work groups of both men and women. These groups are rewarded for their labour with beer, brewed by the holder of the garden and drunk jointly after the work has been completed. This exchange of beer (and sometimes food as well) for labour is called *enyanua* and is an important method of swelling the work force for the more arduous or tedious agricultural tasks. All remaining agricultural work, however, is done exclusively by women.

In addition to the women's gardens, there are certain fields which are cultivated by residential groups under the direction of males. These fields (called *eshiipa* or *ikwila*, depending on the residential group involved) are sown primarily in millets or a cash crop.

Animal Husbandry

As a rule, Safwa conceal information on the number of cattle they possess both from one another and from outsiders. This reticence cannot be explained by a desire to avoid government taxation, for neither at the time this study was made nor under the British were cattle taxed. Nor was there ever a tax based on wealth. Rather, the information is concealed out of a variety of motives concerning the avoidance of neighbours' envy and of appearing to flaunt one's good fortune and power before others. As a result of this practice, data on the cattle holdings of domestic units were difficult to obtain. I would estimate, however, that holdings vary from about two to twelve head per unit, with an average of about five. The number of sheep and goats is probably somewhat higher.

Livestock circulate in the economy primarily as bridewealth and are used for subsistence as well. Cows' milk is either consumed in the household or sold fresh to Asians or Europeans in Itimba, if there is a way of transporting it to them. Although cattle dung is not deliberately used as manure, beasts are grazed on garden plots near houses after harvesting and the droppings hoed under during the ensuing year's cultivation. Animals are usually slaughtered in connection with funerals or ancestor rituals, and the skins may be prepared for use as baby slings or skirts.

[4] Ox-drawn ploughs have come into use in Safwaland only in the last few years. They are used by men primarily for cultivating cash crops in lowland fields.

Hunting

Hunting is mainly an activity of boys and young men. Small rodents and birds are taken by herders, as they watch their charges, usually with clubs or various kinds of snares. Larger game, primarily antelope, are hunted by young men with dogs and spears. A few men own ancient firearms, but these are only rarely used for hunting, because few are licensed and the owners therefore run the risk of substantial fines if caught by a game warden. For the most part, hunting provides only a minor contribution to the Safwa diet.

In summary, the Safwa are subsistence agriculturalists with a basic dependency on sorghum, eleusine, sweet potatoes, and maize. Family units also possess small herds of cattle, sheep, and goats. Meat and milk from these herds, along with small game, supplement the basic vegetable diet.

Participation in the Cash Economy

Different tribes within Safwa territory are involved in the cash economy to varying degrees; indeed even within tribes there are different degrees of involvement, depending on accessibility to markets and main roads, where in the past Asian merchants and today the national food co-operative arranges to pick up and purchase local produce.

The principal cash crops of the area are pyrethrum, wheat, and coffee. Wheat, the major cash crop in the Ipepete area, is usually grown in fields cultivated jointly by members of an extended family. Quite apart from these crops grown specifically for sale (which are usually under the control of men), subsistence crops like potatoes, millet, and legumes may also be sold. These transactions are carried out most frequently by women, and the goods are either bartered or sold. Cash earned from these sales is usually used to purchase clothes or household goods, such as salt, cooking oil, and matches. The extent of participation in these sorts of cash transactions depends primarily on a woman's access to markets or a main road.

The major source of cash in Safwa communities does not come from the sale of agricultural produce, however, but from wage labour. Of the eighty-three adult males in Ipepete (i.e. males around 18 years old and over) almost 81% had worked for wages at some time in their lives, and of the males who had worked, a little over three-quarters were under 40 years of age. During the year 1963, 25% of all Ipepete males held some kind of employment for at least part of the year. One-third of those employed remained in Ipepete and walked to their jobs as messenger, watchman, or labourer in Itimba; two-thirds of those employed were away at jobs, half in the Zambia Copper Belt and half in distant parts of Tanzania.

Over the last fifteen years, the typical work pattern for Ipepete men has been to go to either the Zambian (Northern Rhodesian) or South African mines[5] at about 18 years of age. If the young man's father has met his obligation to supply his son with bridewealth for the first wife, the young man usually leaves after his wife has given birth to their first child. These married men earn wages to acquire another wife. Once they have done so, they rarely absent themselves from home again. Those youths whose fathers cannot pay bridewealth go before marriage to acquire their first wife and may return again to accumulate the wherewithal to acquire a second. A few temporary jobs may be obtained within walking distance of Ipepete either at a government forest reserve or in Itimba with an Asian merchant or government agency. These jobs are sought by some only when money is needed to pay taxes or purchase clothes.

In short, Ipepete men engage in the kind of 'target labour' typical of the African continent.[6] The cash return from this labour is used primarily to obtain either consumer goods, such as clothing, or cattle for bridewealth. The principal sources of these cattle are Sangu, Bungu, or other non-Safwa groups. Other capital goods, such as hoe- or axe-blades are also commonly purchased, and six men in Ipepete had also invested part of their earnings in bicycles, and three men in steel ploughs. The other major expenditure of wages is the head tax, which in 1963 amounted to 60 shillings for every male who was no longer of school age.

We note that, for the most part, cash is used by the Mwanabatnu primarily in dealings with the outside world. Within the indigenous economy, cash circulates mainly in a prestige sphere with women and cattle and is also used to discharge certain social obligations (e.g. buying a cloth to bury with the body of a deceased relative or friend). It is also used to pay diviners. Some craft items, like baskets and hoe handles, may be purchased but are more often traded for other goods. Thus, although a large proportion of males in Ipepete have worked at one time for wages, the uses to which this cash has been put are

[5] Recruiting Tanzanian workers for the South African mines ceased in the early 1960s.

[6] Kamarck (1965) provides a concise summary of research on African labour patterns.

limited mostly to the purchase of consumer goods or to conversion into items in the prestige sphere of the local economy. Capital investment of wages in the national economy is practically non-existent.

SOCIAL STRUCTURE

The following analysis consists of a brief description of the basic relations of incorporation and alliance (Leach 1961:21; Barth 1966: 4, 23-4) in Mwanabantu society. It stresses social structure rather than social organization (Firth 1956) to provide the background for an understanding of the structure of witchcraft and sorcery beliefs.

Relations of Incorporation

With the single exception of the group called the house (*enyumba*), relations of incorporation in Mwanabantu tribe are symbolized in terms of the assistance and protection of the spirits of all ancestors reckoned through males. Thus, apart from the exception cited, all groups are defined by the rights of members to the assistance of named patrilineal forebears in increasing the common substance of the unit as a whole, either through reproduction of offspring or germination of crops. Members also have the right to the ancestors' protection against mystical attack from other members. These rights imply the members' obligation to one another both to contribute to their common substance and to maintain harmony. This latter value is frequently expressed at ancestor rites in the phrase, 'We must be of one heart (intention).'

While this class of incorporative relationships is delimited as a whole by rights and obligations with respect to mystical agents, members of the class are distinguished one from another by rights in corporeal goods—by both the kinds of goods and the precise allocation of rights over these goods. A major differentiation is thus made, on the one hand, between groups that hold property, towards the development of which each member must contribute and from the increase of which each member is entitled to share, and, on the other hand, groups which hold residual rights to certain properties but neither work them jointly nor share in their increase. Although these two classes of groups are not distinguished terminologically by Safwa speakers, we shall call them communal and non-communal groups respectively.

There are two communal groups in Safwa-speaking tribes, the

compound (*exaya*) and the community (*empaɲa*), and two non-communal groups, the patrilineage and tribe (both *eshixɔlɔ* in Safwa, the reason for which will be made obvious shortly). In contrast with this class of groups, the 'house' is based on incorporation not through a descent ideology but through filiation to one woman. Thus, a 'house' consists of all children born of a single genetrix, regardless of the genitor. These children share certain rights and obligations which will be described more fully below.

Communal Groups: The Compound and the Community
The compound and the community differ from one another first in the kind of property each holds. Within the compound the jointly worked property (the *eshiipa*) consists of both land and livestock; within the community it consists of land alone. The major difference between these two units, however, derives not from these structural features but from the organizational features by which they come to contain different proportions of holders of their common constituent statuses. Let us examine these units in some detail.

The Compound. Since the ground plan of a compound which has reached the stage of maximum development in the domestic cycle reflects some of the major principles upon which social statuses are conferred, we begin our discussion of the social structure with a description of this ground plan. Figure 1 represents the plan of a 'typical' example of a compound.[7] A compound consists of a dwelling area and surrounding cultivated fields. A mud plaster yard demarcates the dwelling area from the fields, and in most cases a living fence of euphorbia encloses the dwelling area and separates it from the associated gardens.

The small house standing by itself is that of the compound head (*omwɛnexaya*). It is here that he keeps his personal belongings and spends the night when he is not sleeping with one of his wives. These wives reside, one to a house, in the line of dwellings ranging across the compound. With them live their unmarried daughters and young sons under the age of about eight. The larger building standing by itself is the men's house (*ibanza or empaɲa*) where the older unmarried

[7] This diagram is a copy of one of three, drawn for the investigator by young adult male Safwa. After the 'artists' had completed their work, we questioned them about where they had got the idea for their drawings. Each one reported that it was like his father's compound when he was a boy. Significantly for our present discussion, none of the drawings differed in the kinds of houses depicted, the only major variation being the spatial arrangement of the houses.

An Introduction to Mwanabantu Area

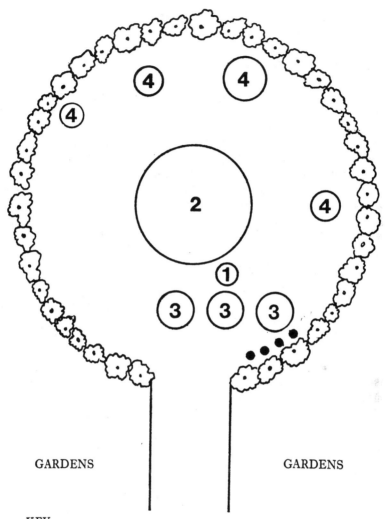

KEY

1 — Compound-head's hut
2 — Men's house (*empaɲa* or *ibanza*)
3 — Houses of compound-head's wives
4 — Houses of wives of the compound-head's sons
● — Granaries

Fig. 1.—Diagram of the ground plan of a compound. Copy of a Safwa drawing. (Key supplied by the author.)

sons stay together with their married brothers, when the latter are not sleeping with their wives. The other houses, scattered haphazardly towards the rear of the compound yard, belong to these wives.

The dimensions on which the resident personnel of a compound are segregated are thus: first, sex; then, within the male sex, generation (as evidenced by the physical separation of the dwellings of the compound head or father and his sons), and within the female sex, full adult status. These dimensions also delimit the assignment of statuses as well. Thus the major statuses are compound head, wife (*onshi*), and inhabitants of the men's house (the *abibanza*), who are divided into 'our children' (*abana kwetu*) and 'stranger-dependants' (*apena*). Stranger-dependants are usually children, either of daughters or sisters of the compound head or of his wives by former husbands. Some, however, are adults, who may join the compound if (1) they can demonstrate either consanguineal or affinal kinship with the compound head[8] and (2) they commit their labour to the family estate.

The family estate (*eshiipa*), consisting of land and livestock, is the focus for relations among the statuses mentioned above. The compound head is responsible for managing the cultivation of gardens and care of livestock. Residents of the young men's house are obliged to work *eshiipa* plots, but their major responsibility is to care for the livestock. For this, they are entitled to bridewealth for obtaining their first wives. (Today, towards the *apena*, this obligation on the part of the compound head is voluntary, and most *apena* therefore secure bridewealth by means of cash earned through absentee labour.) The wives of the compound are obliged to work the *eshiipa* fields and in return receive equal divisions of the *eshiipa* yield. Rights of inheritance in the *eshiipa* also extend equally to the houses to which each of these women gives rise.

In addition to these economic rights and obligations which mesh the statuses within the compound, there are rights and obligations which the compound head has vis-à-vis all dwellers in his compound. First, he is responsible for keeping peace within the residential unit. The following palaver from an ancestor rite underscores this duty clearly. The situation which elicited this interchange was the negligence of a compound head named Mwazozo in seeing to it that his son consulted a diviner over the illness of his child. Although this

---

[8] The one exception to this rule is the occasional practice of permitting young, unrelated males to reside in the compound for a year or so in order to assist with cattle herding.

quotation mentions only children, wives are equally subject to the discipline of the compound head.

[One of the assembled elders speaking.] Now talk with your child. Mwazozo, if he refuses, take your child to the elders [i.e. a council of the community composed of all compound heads, including kin and non-kin of the offending family].

[The leader of the ancestor rite, interrupting the speaker.] Don't tell him to go before the public. When you speak of such matters in public, they should already be settled.

You, friends, if you bear a child, do you take the child before the elders? You say to take him to the people? Do they take a child before the people without questioning him first? Now I have many children. Can I send them before the elders? No, I cannot. When I leave the public meetings, I ask him, 'You, son, aren't you doing your work? If you have stopped, tell me.'

Thus the compound head has primary responsibility for seeing that people within his compound conform to behavioural norms. For this reason Mwazozo is encouraged in this passage to exhaust his own powers of influence before bringing the case to the attention of the village elders. To discipline his dependants, the compound head may use methods from quiet persuasion to physical punishment in the case of younger children and wives. A man who frequently resorts to beatings, however, is considered a poor compound head indeed for thus substituting the strong arm for respect and kindness in order to establish harmony.

The foregoing quotation also points up another duty of the compound head vis-à-vis his dependants: he must consult a diviner should a member of his compound fall ill. There is a close relationship between these two responsibilities in Safwa society, as we shall see in Chapter II when we examine the relationship between deviance and ill-health or death. Indeed both these obligations of the compound head (rule enforcement and consultation of a diviner) may be subsumed under one primary duty of fostering and maintaining order and harmony among compound members.

In addition to these roles which a compound head has with respect to the members of his compound, he also represents the entire compound in political and ritual relations with other compounds. We shall consider these other role sets of the compound head in the sections on the community and patrilineage respectively.

The Community (empaŋa). Flying over Mwanabantu territory, one sees compounds scattered on high ground almost continuously across the countryside. From that vantage point it would be impossible to tell whether the compounds were aggregated into any larger social units, for the next larger unit, the community, is defined entirely by sociological criteria. No precise geographical boundaries differentiate one division from the next. Thus, a community consists of a number of adjacent compounds whose members jointly work certain fields (the *ikwila*) under the direction of a headman (*omwɛnɛ*).

The Concepts of the Community and the Compound. There are two mythical charters for explaining how communities are founded. The first harks back to a time when Mwanabantu territory was inhabited by people who knew neither the use of fire nor the cultivation of millet. These benighted people depended mostly on wild game for food, since they grew only gourds, and ate all food raw. One day a foreigner arrived with eleusine and sorghum seeds and the knowledge of kindling fire with two sticks. So impressed were the aborigines with the stranger's skills and their first taste of cooked meat, that they made him their headman. They still retained their former leader as his assistant, however.

The second charter for the *empaɲa* explains the formation of communities stemming from the original settlement. These derivative communities are said to have been started by descendants of the original headman, who were sent off by their father to settle in particular sectors of the territory. Each of these sons is conceived as going off with a 'friend', not a kinsman, who then became his assistant in the community which gradually grew up around them.

Notably, both these charters establish the community as consisting of three kinds of people: first, the headman (*omwɛnɛ*); second, his assistant (*omwitongwa*); and third, the general public (either called *apena* or *abibanza*). The terms for both the headman and the general public give us a clue about the way in which the organization of the community is conceived, for both these terms obviously derive from statuses within the compound. Thus it will be remembered that the head of a compound is the *omwɛnexaya*, literally the possessor (*omwɛnɛ*) of the compound (*exaya*). *Apena* refers to male residents of a compound who are not patrilineal kinsmen of the compound head, and *abibanza* means literally 'the people of the men's house (*ibanza*)'. The very term used for the community (*empaɲa*) itself is another word for the men's house.

This parallel terminology indicates that the community and the compound are based on the same ideological model. Thus, the headman corresponds terminologically to the compound head, and the general public corresponds to the residents of the men's house, both kinsmen and stranger-dependants. This parallel extends even further: residents of a community cultivate certain fields (the *ikwila*) in common under the direction of the headman, just as the residents of a compound cultivate the *eshiipa* jointly under the compound head. In both cases the yield of the jointly cultivated fields is consumed collectively at ancestor rites; in the compound, for the compound head's ancestors, and in the community, for the headman's ancestors.

The community, in brief, is the compound of the first settler or public benefactor of an area—greatly augmented by 'stranger-dependants', it is true, but a compound nevertheless.[9] This is clearly the conception held throughout the Safwa dialect area, for the community is universally termed the headman's *exaya* (compound) in chiefly ancestor rites throughout this area. Only the headman's assistant lacks a prototype within the compound. We shall now review the major roles associated with the forementioned status categories to show how these parallel those within the compound.

Status Relationships in the Community. Just as the compound head supplies the unifying focus for the various houses of the compound, so the headman unites the disparate compounds of the community and comes to represent the harmony of the whole. When we asked one headman what his duties were, he replied, 'First, to be head of the community. Second, to pray (*-put-*) to the ancestor spirits. And third, to exhort (*-bil-*) the people.' Let us consider each of these duties in turn.

1. To head the community: as head of the community, the *omwεnε*'s major responsibilities are to deal with external affairs, to help settle internal disputes, and to oversee cultivation of the *ikwila*. These roles clearly parallel the major duties of the ordinary compound head.

We shall treat the foreign relations aspect of the headman's role in the section on the tribe. With respect to internal disputes in the community the headman is first among a panel of equals composed of compound heads of senior position in their respective patrilineages. Members of this panel hear cases between compounds, which arise most frequently from elopement or non-payment of bridewealth. They also hear any dispute within a compound which cannot be

[9] Our census data indicate that Safwa communities range in size from about 100 to approximately 1,500 inhabitants, with a mean population of about 580. Invariably the *apena* outnumber the members of the headman's descent group in the community, whereas in the normal compound they never exceed 20% of the total population of residents.

settled satisfactorily either by its head or by a mediator who may be called in *ad hoc* for marital disputes. In the past any witchcraft case in which a member of the headman's family was involved, either as a culprit or victim, also had to be heard by the headman and elders.

It is noteworthy that this manner of settling disputes through judicial means before a panel of equals differs from most dispute settlement in the compound, which is handled through a precisely graded allocation of authority by generation and, within generations, by relative age. Within the compound there is thus a clear chain of command from the compound head down to his youngest son. One of the differences between statuses in the compound and in the community is thus this absence of hierarchy in the community among compound heads of different descent groups. (Compound heads of the same descent group would of course be graded hierarchically in terms of generation and relative age, as they are within the compound.)

In these judicial cases in the community the effort of the elders is bent on reconciling the antagonists, not on administering punishment —a procedure which is reminiscent of the value placed on harmony in the compound as well. Part of the success of the elders depends upon the timing of their intervention in the dispute, and this is largely the headman's decision. In the past all successfully closed cases were marked by a feast in which a goat or chicken was supplied by the guilty party for all to eat as a sign of mutual agreement. This custom has been abandoned, however. Some disputes in the community which are not settled satisfactorily by judicial means are referred to divinatory processes, as we shall see.[10]

Another part of the peace-keeping role of headman is to act as witness to agreements concerning bridewealth and inheritance. He must also be present at all funerals before the corpse is buried, in order to act as witness and interpreter of the autopsy. As we shall see, the occasion of a death may be a time not only for bringing up old grudges but also for possibly settling them.

As director of work in the *empaŋa*'s communal fields, the headman chooses sites for cultivation and gives orders when the various tasks in preparation of the plots should be performed. Furthermore, residents of the community are not supposed to perform these same tasks on their own fields until they have been ordered to do so on the communal fields. Thus the compound heads of a community are not

---

[10] See Gluckman (1962:450–1) for a more lengthy discussion of the distinction between these two mechanisms of social control.

supposed to burn off or harvest their own *eshiipa* fields until the headman has begun doing so to the *ikwila*. Individual field-holders in turn are not supposed to start these activities until their compound head has begun. In this way the headman controls the major activities of the agricultural calendar within his community.

2. To pray to the ancestor spirits: we shall discuss the role of the ancestor spirits in greater depth in the following chapter. For the present, however, we note that they are conceived as protecting their descendants against disease or death and that a headman's ancestors are believed in addition to have special control over the weather, which is conceived by many Safwa-speakers as a manifestation of the principal divinity. Thus reference to the wind is equivalent in some contexts to mention of *Ongolobɛ* ('God').

Because of this key role of the headman's ancestral spirits, it is considered particularly important for them to be remembered in ancestor rituals. Thus the harvest from a community's *ikwila* fields is used to prepare the beer for annual memorial rites, which are held after the main harvest in June. The headman's ancestors are also appealed to if the rains fail to begin at the expected time or the quantity exceeds optimum limits. Thus, although members of the community are not all patrilineal kin of the headman, they become involved in rites to his ancestors, as though they were kin, through participation in the cultivation of the grain used for the ceremonial beer.

3. To exhort the people: whenever the people of a community gather together, it is the headman's duty to sermonize about the importance of peace and to urge the residents to lay aside their grudges. Through these exhortations, through his role in settling disputes and organizing communal labour, and through his roles as descendant of the ancestors who weld the community into a congregation, the headman comes to represent in his own person the solidarity and unity of the group itself.

The rights and prerogatives which set a headman off from other elders are few. Materially he is not better off and must cultivate his own fields like any commoner. The only special right which he exercises is to receive a basket of beer at any occasion when the beverage is served. Since beer-drinking is an occasion when disputes are often aired and settled informally before they reach serious proportions, this special privilege is functionally efficacious in ensuring that the headman will be present when such matters arise. In the past headmen were also entitled to all women taken in raids on other communities. As a matter of external relations, however, this privilege will be discussed in the section on the tribe below.

The Status of Assistant (omwitɔŋwa) and the Acquisition of Land in the Community. All petitions for land by potential settlers must be addressed to the headman's assistant, who is custodian of the land. Any such petitioner who is known to be generous and peaceful may be given a house site in the community. With the house site go rights to cultivate the land surrounding it and any other lands in the vicinity of the community not already claimed by previous residents. Rights to these unclaimed lands are activated through cultivation and, once activated, may be passed inviolate to anyone the cultivator wishes. Only if the holder is driven out of the community or ceremonially renounces his claim to the land may someone else cultivate it without his permission. If a man moves out of the community voluntarily, he may still retain and exercise his rights to cultivate there. If he is not using the land himself, he may lend it to someone else until he wishes it back. If he does not wish to retain claim to the land, he announces this publicly at a special beer feast and the land reverts to the stewardship of the headman. The headman and his assistant may then reallocate the land in any way they see fit, since it once again becomes a part of the headman's family estate (*ikwila*).

The Community: A Summary. As we have seen, the community is conceived as the vastly expanded compound of the descendant of the first settler or culture hero. Just as an ordinary compound head may bring in stranger-dependants (*apena*) to settle in his enclosure and provide them with gardens, so the headman allows strangers to settle within his midst and lay claim to uncultivated land. And just as the compound head retains reversionary rights to granted land, so, too, does the headman. In addition, just as the residents of a compound jointly cultivate certain fields, the harvest of which is used in part to brew beer for the compound head's ancestors, so community dwellers cultivate together to produce beer for the headman's forebears. And just as the compound head represents the compound to other members of the community and is responsible for the maintenance of harmony within his compound, so the headman represents his community vis-à-vis other communities and is responsible for maintaining peace among its members.

The major differences between the community and the compound are: (1) only land constitutes the jointly worked resource in the community, while both land and livestock are so worked in the compound;

(2) the number of stranger-dependants (*apena*) far exceeds the number of patrilineal kin of the headman in the community but does not even approach an equal ratio in the compound; and (3) judicial means of settling disputes are typically employed within the community but are used within the compound only for marital disputes. Apart from these rather superficial differences, the social structure of the compound and of the community are, in sum, the same.

This does not mean that in some contexts these units are not differentiated, however. In Chapter IV we shall see that, with respect to notions about disputes and the aetiology of disease, they clearly are.

Non-Communal Groups: The Patrilineage and the Tribe
The Patrilineage (*eshixɔlɔ*). We defined non-communal groups as those in which the members do not work a common property and share in its increase. The patrilineage is such a group which comes about in the course of the developmental cycle of the compound. Thus, in the developmental cycle, the sons of the compound head move away when their oldest male children reach 8 to 10 years of age. On moving, a son's obligation to work the family estate and his right to receive a share of its yield become attenuated. The degree of attenuation depends on where the son settles, but there is a tendency for him to remain near enough to continue to help work the father's *eshiipa*. Furthermore, a son can conveniently exercise the rights to cultivate fields which will pass to him on the death of his father only if he remains in the general vicinity of his father's lands.

In spite of the proximity in which brothers may live, however, there are really very few economic obligations which they owe one another, except jointly with respect to their father. Half-brothers are not responsible for one another's bridewealth, and uterine brothers bear joint responsibility only for the bridewealth of one another's first marriages. In addition, brothers need not contribute towards the bridewealth of their patrilineal nephews. Nor are they obliged to keep either the *eshiipa* or incoming bridewealth property intact. They may sustain a co-operative economic relationship if it is mutually advantageous to them to do so, but it is not an essential part of their roles as brothers. Whether or not brothers maintain themselves as a co-operative and property-holding unit either after the dispersal stage of the domestic cycle or after the death of their father thus depends on factors of social organization, not of social structure.

Even if brothers subdivide their father's *eshiipa*, however, they still retain residual rights in the *eshiipa* property. These rights form one of the bases of the patrilineage. Thus, stemming from these residual rights, members of a patrilineage may ask one another for fields or cattle for bridewealth. In fact, rights to cattle are rarely honoured even among brothers, as we have pointed out. Rights to fields, however, may be retained for several generations. This permits members of a patrilineage to acquire fields from collaterals and thereby alleviate discrepancies in man-land relations arising from the greater size of one segment over another.

The shallowness of genealogies in Mwanabantu tribe attests, however, to the general availability of land and absence of the necessity to retain these ties. With the exception of the patrilines of headmen, genealogies are generally not reckoned beyond the grandparental generation of the adult members of the society.[11] Groups of this genealogical depth become 'convening groups' (to use Goody's phrase, 1961:5), in which the members assemble for rites to their forebears but do not often activate rights to fields.

In short, the patrilineage is a natural outgrowth of the developmental cycle of the compound. Its incorporative basis may shift, in time, from both residual rights in common property and a mystical tie to the mystical tie only. This mystical tie brings the patrilineal descendants of an apical ancestor together to honour their forebears and to request their protection and assistance in maintaining harmony and fertility. Final dissolution and disregard of a patrilineal tie is signalled by non-attendance at these rites.

[11] In the process of collecting genealogies of the heads of compounds in Ipepete, we recorded data on fifteen different lineages. Beside the headman's lineage, we encountered only five lineages in which members could reckon ancestors beyond their grandfathers. Even then, only the names of men in the direct line of descent were remembered. In two lineages these names extended three generations beyond the grandparental; in one lineage, two; and in two lineages, only one generation.

The reasons given by members of these particular lineages about why they 'remembered' links in excess of the typical two generations are informative about Safwa society. Two of the lineages retained the links because they were immigrants into Magombe area in the past generation and would need to re-establish kin connections should they wish to return to their former homes. Two other lineages retained memory of the early links because of their importance in the history of the settlement of the area, one lineage claiming to have arrived in Ipepete with the first member of the present line of headmen and the other asserting that they had occupied the area since time immemorial. We do not know any reason why the fifth lineage recalled ancestors beyond the third generation. All four of the lineages, whose reasons for remembering remote ancestors we know, did so for social or economic considerations, as previous work on the use of genealogies would lead us to suspect (e.g. McLennan 1896; Gulliver 1955; Winter 1956; Needham 1966).

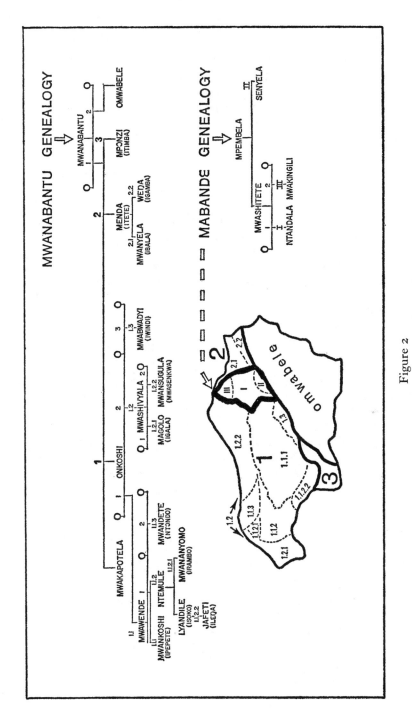

Figure 2

Mwanabantu and Mabande tribal genealogies and the geographical location of tribal segments; names in parentheses under the genealogical names are the geographical designations of the areas inhabited by each segment

The Tribe. Communities, we have seen, are conceived as expanded, chiefly compounds. Understandably, therefore, relations between communities are conceptually equivalent to relations between compounds. That is, communities inter-relate through the same patrilineal idiom as do some compounds. Indeed the term in the Safwa language for patrilineage is the same as the one which we are also translating here as 'tribe' (*eshixɔlɔ*).

A tribe is thus a number of communities linked through the patrilineal ties of their headmen into a segmentary system. Figure 2 shows the segmentary patrilineal organization of Mwanabantu tribe. Although relationships among communities are very similar qualitatively to relationships among the segments of a patrilineage, quantitatively the number of contexts in which communities interact is much less than those in which members of the same patrilineage interact. Today these contexts are limited almost entirely to ancestor rites for members of the chiefly lineage, rites prompted by phenomena believed to be influenced by chiefly ancestors (e.g. rain or epidemics), and disputes which cut across community boundaries.

In the past, however, warfare provided an important context for the interaction of segments. Warfare between segments seems to have centred around the theft of cattle and women. When these possessions were stolen, the entire community was responsible for avenging the theft, and anyone living in the community of the thief became subject to retribution. In the course of the resultant raiding and counter-raiding between segments, the headman would appropriate wives for himself.

The fact that warfare occurred between segments in the past, in defiance of the value of lineage unity, suggests that genealogical lines were much more fluid in the past than at present. There are a number of additional lines of evidence to support this observation.

First, in skirmishes genealogical proximity never determined alliance, as it reportedly does in other segmentary systems. (See, for example, Sahlins's review of the characteristics of segmentary societies; 1961:331–2.) On the contrary, our information indicates that when two genealogically close segments were disputing, each side might woo more distant segments to come to their aid against their near kinsmen. Thus in the early 1920s when Mwankoshi (1.1.1 in Figure 2) was having a dispute with his brother Ntemule (1.1.2), he persuaded his much more distant kinsmen, the descendants of Menda (2) to come to his aid. From all indications alliances of this nature were not anomalous, and thus friendly relations between segments were not strictly determined by genealogical proximity.

Second, evidence of genealogical adjustments arising out of hostility and warfare may be found in historical information provided by Kootz-Kretschmer. The autobiography of Mlotwa (1929:II, 196) even supplies an example from Mwanabantu territory. After a skirmish in which Mwanabantu was driven out by his grandson, the narrator is quoted as saying that the two kinsmen 'fingen an sich zu hassen, und in dem Haas ging die Verwandtschaft unter'. Thus genealogical relationships within tribes did adjust rather readily to social factors.

In short, the tribe is basically the same kind of group as the lineage, with its activities, however, limited to chiefly ancestor rites and the divinatory settlement of disputes between communities of the same tribe. We shall discuss these activities more fully in Chapters II, IV, and V.

The House (enyumba)
The house is the one corporate relationship not based on patrilineal descent. Instead, a house consists of all the children of one woman who have been legitimated by the same bridewealth. Thus, whether the genitor of the children is one man or a succession of brothers who have inherited the same woman, the children all constitute a single 'house'. The genetrix thus constitutes the focus of this social relationship.

The mother of the house is primarily responsible for producing the food for its members. To do this, she cultivates fields which she may acquire in any of three ways: (1) from both her father-in-law and husband at marriage, (2) from her mother or her own patrilineage, and (3) from her own efforts in clearing plots from unclaimed bush. When a woman becomes too old to cultivate, she may cede the fields acquired in the first manner to her sons' wives, thus keeping them in her husband's patrilineage. Those obtained from her own patrilineage she usually returns to some younger member, if they are needed. Otherwise she may dispose of these fields, along with those she started herself, in any manner she chooses; most often they pass to her daughters. Thus house members stand as a unit by sharing either primary or residual rights to fields worked by their mother.

In addition, the house stands as a unit with respect to the exclusive rights which uterine brothers share in the bridewealth of their uterine sisters.[12] It is these rights which set full brothers apart most sharply from their half-brothers with whom, as we have seen, they share as equals in the land and livestock of their fathers.

Although all full brothers have an equal claim on the bridewealth of their sisters, the oldest unmarried brother has first rights to use this bridewealth for himself. He is not entitled to sell or dispose of the livestock in any other way but to obtain his first wife, however. If for some reason he does not wish to exercise this right, he may cede it to the next unmarried brother. If he wishes to use the bridewealth for anything other than obtaining a wife, however, he must secure the consent of all his brothers, plus his mother and father. To marry, though, he needs his choice of mate approved by his parents only.

This allocation of rights in sisters' bridewealth leads to the conception of an ideal house as one in which there is an equal number of male and female children, born alternately. Under these circumstances a male child would have a sister near his age, who could be married off around the time he requires bridewealth for his own wife. Needless to say, this ideal fails to be fulfilled quite frequently, with the result that some houses have either more or less livestock than they need.

One way in which this inequality may be rectified is by transferring livestock from one house to another. This is done, however, only if all concerned—particularly the founding mothers of the houses—consent. Furthermore, all such livestock must be returned, and strict accounting is kept of these loans. The reasons behind this strict reciprocity between houses will become apparent when we discuss transactional relations.

A loan of bridewealth between houses, while possible, is undesirable to the Safwa, who claim that strife is an almost inevitable accompaniment of these loans. Besides, there are other ways of overcoming a discrepancy between incoming and outgoing cattle within the house. Both the father's *eshiipa* stock and, today, money earned in jobs may be used to provide additional livestock. As a result, only a small number of marriages in Mwanabantu area involved goods borrowed between houses.

Even if cattle are not loaned across house boundaries, however, discrepancies in the number of cattle can cause strife among brothers of different houses, simply because of the unequal numbers of live-

[12] Rights in a sister's bridewealth extend not only to the cattle actually received for her, but also to any increase which may come from these animals. This wider definition applies throughout our subsequent discussion.

stock to which the brothers can lay claim. Thus, a man who has many brothers and few sisters within his house may look with jealousy upon his bridewealth-rich half-brother who has many sisters and no brothers. This was certainly a cause of one of the two cases of notorious disharmony between half-brothers which existed in Ipepete.

During the stage of the domestic cycle when all the brothers reside within the father's compound, the house is not only a category of actors in the social system but a property-holding group as well. Later, however, when the individual brothers go off to establish their own compounds and the house thus becomes dispersed geographically, any livestock remaining from their sisters' bridewealth may be divided equally among them. In some houses, on the other hand, the brothers still maintain joint control over this property even after they have dispersed. Similarly the cattle and lands which come to the house as a unit on the death of the father may either be subdivided among the male members or continue to be held jointly. Which course of action will be followed in both these cases depends primarily on how far apart the brothers settle, which depends in turn on ecological and other conditions.

In conclusion, a house constitutes a strictly defined and bounded category of people in the social system: all the children of one woman who have been legitimated by the same bridewealth. These people share rights to inherit fields cultivated by the woman who bore them; in addition, the males of the unit share exclusive rights to the bridewealth of the females and inherit jointly from the *eshiipa* of their father.

Potentially, therefore, the males of a house form a property-holding unit as well as a socially defined category. Whether the brothers in fact exercise their rights to the property jointly or not depends on the particular stage of the domestic cycle through which the group is passing. Thus when the brothers reside together in their father's compound, they hold property jointly. Later, however, when they disperse to found compounds of their own, the property may be divided equally among them. Each brother may then control the use of his own share independently of the rest. Thus, at this stage of the cycle some houses cease to be property-holding units. Other houses, however, do not distribute the joint property until some time later, after the father has died.

In relations between houses, an ethic of strict reciprocity prevails in striking contrast to the ethic of sharing and unity which characterizes life in the men's house. The bond between the children of different mothers, when their status as children of mothers is focal, would seem to be something quite different from their incorporative relationship as children of the same father. The former bond is a transactional one, and we shall discuss it further below.

Relations of Incorporation: A Summary

Basically, relations of incorporation are conceived in terms of the mystical protection and assistance of named patrilineal forebears. This mystical unity, which is demonstrated in ancestor rites, constitutes the minimal expression of incorporation in Mwanabantu society. Various economic rights and obligations may also be connected with this mystical tie, but these economic aspects of the incorporative relationship become gradually attenuated with increasing generational removal from the common ancestor. Thus, within two generations' removal from the founding ancestor, most patrilineages in Mwanabantu area become merely convening groups which assemble to express their unity with respect to the ancestors. These rites and the nature of this unity will be described more fully in the following chapter.

Relations of Transaction

Although transactional relations have already been mentioned in our discussion of the strict reciprocity which characterizes relations between houses, the mutual prestations which mark the marital tie best exemplify this mode of interaction.

Marriage in Mwanabantu tribe often grows out of relations between trading partners (*abinɛ*; singular, *omwinɛ*). *Abinɛ* are always non-kinsmen, usually from different tribes and different ecological niches, who maintain an exchange of uncooked food between one another. In any year either partner may go to the other to solicit food if he is short, with the understanding that he is obligated to the giver to return an equivalent when asked. Only certain foods are considered equivalent in this kind of exchange; for example, peas are interchangeable for beans or wheat for millet, but peas and millet are not ordinarily exchanged. Although not all marriage negotiations grow out of a relationship of this kind, the parties to a marriage relation are known as *abinɛ* during the initial stages of the arrangement, and this term thus expresses the reciprocal nature of the relationship.

A series of ceremonial exchanges punctuates the relationships between the kinsmen of a bride and groom, and we shall review these briefly to get a better idea of the nature of transactional relationships in Mwanabantu society.

1. There are three major ways of initiating a marriage contract, and the content of the first exchanges varies with these ways. We shall here describe only the method which is most common today (*asipanɛ*). The initiative for marriage by this method comes from the couple themselves. Initial overtures by the male are accompanied by gifts of 1 or 2 shillings to the girl. When the girl consents to marry, the boy, after telling his father, goes with an older brother or father's brother to his intended's father with a hoe. After presenting the gift, they announce their intention; the girl is called and, if she publicly consents to the union, is given a special gift by her fiancé (*ohɔlɛlɔ*, usually 20 shillings). The amount of bridewealth to be paid before the next meeting is then announced, and the bride's family serves beer and perhaps food as well. An important point to note is that the father of the girl does not speak directly to the boy's representative but through an intermediary. The role of intermediary, who also acts as witness, is extremely important in all transactional relations in this society.

2. After this meeting the groom begins bride-service for his intended's parents. He is given two major tasks: (1) to cultivate a field for his father-in-law and (2) to build a house for his mother-in-law. (The latter task may be called for whenever the mother-in-law wishes and may be delayed for several years.) The bride also begins service for her future husband's family, carrying firewood and water for her mother-in-law. She is also given several fields to cultivate from her husband's lineage lands and starts working in her father-in-law's *eshiipa* instead of her own father's.

3. When the first bridewealth payment has been met, the parents and siblings of the bride brew beer and have a brief consultation with the parents and siblings of the groom. At this meeting the total amount of livestock to be given as bridewealth is set, as well as the number which are to be paid before the next major ceremony ('the beer of the in-laws'). By the time of this first small ceremony, a special sheep (the *eshixɔnɔ*), which is given to the bride's mother's brother, will have been presented.

4. The next set of prestations (*embɔnɔlɔ*), which will not be described in detail, are given by the groom in exchange for sexual rights in his fiancée.

5. When the stipulated number of bridewealth animals has been provided, the bride's lineage brews about 50 gallons of beer for the groom's lineage. Then one of the major marriage ceremonies occurs, the 'beer of the in-laws' (*ehɔmbwa eyaxɔyi*). This ceremony is marked by numerous prestations of animals, cash, and cloths for the bride's kin, and food and beer for the groom's.
6. Meanwhile, as soon as the fields which the bride has been cultivating at her father-in-law's have been harvested and the groom has provided his wife with a suitable dwelling, the girl takes up residence with her husband in his father's compound. Thenceforth she sends cooked food to the men's house every day.
7. Beginning with ceremony 1, the bride avoids any member of her husband's lineage who stands in the relationship of father, father's sister, or older brother to her husband. These tabus are lifted with members of the older-brother category when they pay the bride a sum of money, usually 2 shillings.
8. After the birth of the couple's first child, the immediate families of both parents assemble at the girl's mother's hut. Both the girl's and boy's mothers prepare beer for the occasion; this is the first time that both sides offer the same gift in exchange. The father of the boy also kills a goat, which the assembled families eat. From then on the parents-in-law are no longer termed *abinɛ* but *alyambuzi*, 'those who have eaten goat.' At this ceremony the child is given one name from the patrileages of each of its parents, again stressing the mutuality of the relationship which produced the offspring.
9. After the child walks, the wife brews a special beer for her father-in-law to end the strict avoidance between them.

This somewhat lengthy list of prestations and counter-prestations is included here to show the reciprocal character of transactional relationships. We note that initially the alliance entails an exchange of different commodities, but as it becomes more and more an incorporative relationship, the prestations become identical. Thus at the ceremony marking the birth of the child, both sets of parents supply beer for the first time.

This kind of mutual exchange is not limited to affinal relations alone, however. Relations between tribes may be governed by the same kind of transactions. Thus another tribe was 'wife' to Mwanabantu tribe, and in return for that tribe's control over fertility through their influence on rain, the Mwanabantu sent them gifts of cloth, hoes, and occasionally cattle.[13]

Relations between the ethnographer and residents of Ipepete began as strictly reciprocal ones. Initially, people brought eggs or chickens for medicines or other favours. In time, however, these prestations ceased, and one inhabitant of Ipepete remarked how difficult my life must be with all these people asking for favours and without any kinsmen to help me refuse them. In other words, I was in the unenviable position of being treated like everyone's kinsman, since I had none of my own. As I began participating in the life of the community, I was thus involved by the residents as much as possible in incorporative relations, since my greater wealth saved me from calling on the people of Ipepete for material assistance, and the incorporative mode saved them the cost of the prestations required by a transactional relationship. I, too, benefited by this incorporation of course by becoming privy to more information.

Summary and Conclusions

Social relations in Mwanabantu tribe are thus characterized on the one hand, by incorporative relations carried out in an idiom of patrilineal descent and an ethic of sharing and unity, and, on the other hand, by transactional relations carried out in an idiom of exchange and an ethic of reciprocity. The contrast between these two kinds of social relations is shown most dramatically among sons of different houses. These men, while acting as sons of the same father and thus as patrilines, share property, labour, quarters, and food; as children of different mothers and thus as non-agnates, however, these same men exchange goods (usually bridewealth) only with due attention to strict reciprocity.

Although these are the major structural features of Mwanabantu society, they may be modified by solutions to organizational problems. This is particularly true for incorporative relations, which initially are very close and embrace activities in a number of spheres. In time, however, demographic and ecological factors promote dispersion of actors linked in this kind of relationship, and with this dispersion comes an attenuation of economic obligations, leaving only moral and ritual ties. In the following chapter we shall investigate these ties and their relation to disease and death.

[13] This relationship is reminiscent of the institution of perpetual kinship described by Cunnison among the Luapula peoples (1956).

CHAPTER II

DISEASE, DEATH, DEVIANCE, AND THE ANCESTORS

In the previous chapter we described the social system of Mwanabantu tribe as a background to our analysis of the relationship between social discord and the aetiology of disease and death (*empongo*). The present chapter serves as a bridge to this analysis and, looking ahead, prepares the way for an investigation of the semantics of the aetiology of *empongo* by describing the systematic relationship which exists in Safwa thought among the elements *empongo*, the ancestor spirits, and certain categories of human action which we shall translate as 'deviant behaviour'. At the same time, however, this chapter looks backward; for by explicating the relationship among these three concepts, it furthers comprehension of the mystical tie which forms the basis of the incorporative social relations described in the previous chapter.

The first part of the present chapter discusses the concept of *empongo*, revealing how the disparate ideas of disease and death in English coalesce into one concept in Safwa thought. The second and larger portion is devoted to an exposition of the moral implications of *empongo*, as revealed in ancestor rituals.

THE CONCEPT OF *EMPONGO*

In Safwa ontology every living being and every object possesses an *inzyongoni*, the power or force of existence. In humans the *inzyongoni*, which is conceived as akin to heat, receives the male semen and female vaginal secretions at the time of conception. The foetus is believed to be fashioned from the latter two ingredients and to be expelled from the womb by the force of the *inzyongoni*.

During a person's lifetime his *inzyongoni* may depart from his body either temporarily during sleep or illness or permanently at death. When the *inzyongoni* departs temporarily, the form which remains is referred to as *sigaba*, literally a non-being. (Etymologically this word comes from *sig-*, the negative prefix, plus a form of the verb *-b-*, 'be'

IA Community in the foothills of the Mbeya range, showing dispersed settlement pattern

B Grave of a child who died within the previous month of *empongo embibi*

IIA *Empeta*, dance performed at the ceremony for welcoming a dead person to the White Place, the land of the ancestors

B Arriving at an ancestor ceremony. The man and woman (*centre*) are bringing supplies for the ceremony while the others dance out to greet them

Disease, Death, Deviance, and the Ancestors

or 'become'.) We first heard this term murmured by a diviner after he had palpated and sniffed his patient; he later explained that the person's *inzyongoni* was ebbing from his body. Similarly the form of a person whose *inzyongoni* has departed temporarily in sleep is also termed *sigaba*.

Dying, however, is conceived as a permanent departure of the *inzyongoni* from the body. In the case of permanent departure, the *inzyongoni* travels to the White Place (the realm of the ancestor spirits) and there becomes an *onzimu*, an ancestor spirit. In some cases, however, instead of travelling to the White Place the *inzyongoni* re-enters its bodily residence and thereby causes the person to resume his former qualities and appearance. Three times during our stay with the Safwa, people were reported to have been re-animated (*-zyosh-*) in this way. Once this reportedly occurred while the patient was on his deathbed; the other two times, when the bodies were already in their graves—one a full two weeks after burial.

In short, both disease and death are conceived by the Safwa as resulting from the same phenomenon: the departure or weakening of the *inzyongoni*. Whereas we think of disease and death as essentially different phenomena, albeit causally related in some circumstances, the Safwa envisage a continuous process in the withdrawal or debilitation of the *inzyongoni*. This withdrawal, however, can range from temporary or slight (situations which we would categorize as sleep or sickness) to permanent (death). This serves to clarify the meaning of the term *empongo*. Disease and death, the glosses provided for this term above, are clearly only its *denotata*. The *significatum* of *empongo* is a weakening or withdrawal of the *inzyongoni*, ranging in duration from temporary to permanent.[1] The withdrawal of the *inzyongoni* does not happen to a person without cause, however. It is this cause which we shall explore in the following section through an analysis of ancestor rituals.

---

[1] The concept of the *inzyongoni*, as found among Safwa-speakers, and the concept of 'life force', ascribed by Tempels (1959) to all 'Bantus', are obviously similar in many respects. Since I did not read Tempels until after I returned from the field, however, I had no way of checking on specific similarities and differences in belief.

THE GENERAL CAUSES OF *EMPONGO* AS REVEALED IN ANCESTOR RITES

This section is divided into two parts. The first, which serves as a background to the second, describes the performance of ancestor rites (*emputɔ*; singular, *ɔluputɔ*). The second part examines the verbal content of these rites with the aim of answering the principal problem of this section: what do Safwa conceive the general causes of *empongo* to be?

A Description of Ancestor Rites

Ancestor rites are performed on the following occasions:

Funerary rites.—Prayers to the ancestors are offered as part of the final funerary rite (the *omwɛngulɔ*), which is held for all adults who leave living descendants. The *omwɛngulɔ*, which usually takes place following the first harvest after the deceased's burial, serves to welcome the deceased to the land of the ancestor spirits.

Illness (empongo).—*Emputɔ* may be held when a diviner has named an ancestor responsible for causing the illness of one or more of his descendants.

Igandyɔ ceremony.—Annually, some time after the major millet crop is harvested in June, each headman holds a ceremony in the sacred grove (*igandyɔ*) where those of his ancestors who served as headmen are buried. At this ceremony prayers are said at the graves of all those men who were founders of important segments of the lineage.

'*To show the ancestor spirits we have not forgotten them.*'—The 'etic' situations which provoke this 'emic' statement of a reason for holding an *ɔluputɔ* are the following: (1) when there have been unsettled disagreements or a lack of co-operation among members of a lineage, or (2) when the courses of treatment prescribed by diviners for a sick member of the lineage have failed to effect a cure.

Because ancestor ceremonies require certain paraphernalia which take some time to prepare (beer, for example), preliminary rites may be held with only a few of the necessary props in order to announce to the ancestor spirits the advent of a full-scale ceremony. Cases of illness (when it is particularly important to demonstrate as soon as possible that the ancestors are remembered) and delays in holding scheduled ancestor ceremonies (i.e. the funerary and *igandyɔ* rites) may both occasion these annunciatory rituals.

The Performance of Ancestor Rites

Setting.—The celebrants congregate at the grave of an ancestor to perform the *oluputɔ*. Which ancestor this will be depends on the reason for holding the ceremony. When occasioned by funerary ritual, it is naturally held at the grave of the deceased; in case of illness, at the grave of the ancestor deemed responsible. On all other occasions the ceremony is held at the grave of the founder of the lineage segment immediately concerned in the issue which occasions the rite. Thus if two half-brothers are not getting along well, they 'remember' their ancestors at their father's grave; on the other hand, if headmen from various minor segments of a lineage congregate in the sacred grove for the annual ceremony, they pray at the grave of each grandsire who gave rise to a segment.

Paraphernalia.—The ancestor spirits are addressed through two holes dug at the head of the grave either with a long-handled spoon (*utihɔ*), normally used for stirring porridge, or an archaic bladed tool (*isula*), which was formerly used for harvesting millet.

During the prayers various foods are placed in and around the two holes. Among these are millet flour and millet beer. The feathers of a white fowl are also placed beside the holes. The sex of this fowl must correspond to that of the ancestor at whose grave the rite is being celebrated. A sheep or cow, also of the same sex as the deceased, is killed before the ceremony begins; the liver, thymus, and flesh around the sternum are reserved for the ritual. The remainder of the sacrificial animal is divided among those present. The manner of apportioning it depends on the number of people present at the rite, although certain allotments are standard. Headmen receive ribs, non-kinsmen to the celebrants are guaranteed at least a leg and the entrails, and the donor of the animal always receives the head and skin. The entrails are cooked and eaten at the site, but all other portions of meat are carried home for redistribution and consumption there.

Participants.—Among the participants in an ancestor rite a major distinction is made between the 'living' (*abapansi*; literally 'those of the earth') and those of the realm of the ancestor spirits (*abahuzɛlu*; literally 'those at the White Place'). All participants, however, belong to the grammatical class of persons—a category which has semantic significance as well as grammatical. This assertion is supported by the fact that a person (*omuntu*), who by Safwa standards ceases to act in ways appropriate to humans, may be removed from the personal class and referred to with the prefix of another grammatical class, viz. *ilintu*.

The living participants are divided into *aholo*, 'kinsmen', and *abibanza*, 'the general public'. Without going into details of the kinship system, it may be noted that for purposes of ancestor rites the major categories of kinsmen are: members of the lineage, wives of the lineage, parents of wives of the lineage (*alyambuzi*), and husbands of women of the lineage (*abalamu*).

The participants from the realm of the ancestor spirits are called the *azimu* (singular, *onzimu*), the ancestor spirits themselves. These are divided into the *abalyapayɔ* and all other deceased Safwa. The *abalyapayɔ* are those who died through violence either in war or in a disfiguring accident. The term itself means 'those who eat separately', and the significance of this epithet will become apparent shortly, when we discuss the procedure for conducting the ancestor ceremony. There is no cover term in Safwa for all the other ancestor spirits, and in fact the entire population of deceased Safwa never participate as a group in any ancestor ceremony. Only the antecedents of the living who have come together for a particular ceremony are believed to be present. Certain of these are invoked by name: (1) the ancestor at whose grave the ceremony is being held; (2) his or her spouse(s); (3) the male lineal ancestors of those performing the rite as far back as can be remembered (which is usually to the second generation preceding living adults of the lineage); and (4) the immediate male forebear of people assembled from the various categories of kinsmen distinguished above.

Most pagan Safwa view the ancestor spirits as intermediaries who relay the supplications of the living, which are spoken at the *oluputɔ*, to a being called *Ongolobɛ*—an activity which parallels the role relationship between the headman's assistant and his headman. *Ongolobɛ*, which is the term used by the first Christian missionaries to translate their concept of God into the Safwa dialect, is looked upon in two different ways by Safwa today. Some people view *Ongolobɛ* as the eternal creator of life, water, trees, land, and sky. They clearly differentiate him from the ancestor spirits, who created neither land nor water but once walked the earth, died, and were buried. Other pagans, however, conceive *Ongolobɛ* not as a timeless creator but as another ancestor spirit. For them he is the leading headman in the land of the ancestor spirits, a belief which is born out in prayers by the frequently enunciated instructions for ancestors to 'arise early and go to the headman (*Labele hwamwɛnɛ*)'. For people of this latter persuasion creation is simply accepted as a fact beyond comprehension and of little importance. For neither group of believers, however, is *Ongolobɛ* a direct participant in ancestor rites, although he is often the one who ultimately responds to the suppliants' pleas.[2]

Procedure.—The area around the head of the ancestor's grave is cleared off by the assistant officiant, while the kinsmen of the deceased assemble around the site. All celebrants face the direction in which the deceased has been buried, a fact which is known by his lineage membership. Most lineages in the Magombe area face their dead south towards Itete, the reputed home of the headmen; however, a few lineages face other locations.

After the grave has been cleared and the celebrants assembled, two holes are dug by the assistant: a small one on the right, about 5 inches in diameter, for the *abalyapayɔ* and a larger one on the left, about 3 inches wider, for the other ancestor spirits. The holes and the cleared area surrounding them are known as the *eshipɔnyɔ*, 'the pouring place', or the *eshiputɔ*, 'the praying place'. The assistant sprinkles three lines of millet flour on the *eshipɔnyɔ*, one between the two holes and the other two on the outside edges of the holes. The meat which has been reserved for the ancestors from the sacrificial animal is then taken up by the assistant, and small pieces are distributed to representatives of the major branches of the officiating lineage and their *alyambuzi* (the parents of women married to males of the lineage). The remainder is placed around the holes for the ancestor spirits (Plates IIIa and b).

While this is taking place, several men and women—usually kinsmen of the deceased but occasionally others as well—take some of the ceremonial beer into their mouths and blow it out as they dance and

[2] Besides the obvious parallel between the concept of *Ongolobɛ* as timeless creator and the Christian concept of God, there is other evidence which indicates that this notion may not be indigenous. First, almost all people who hold the second view, that *Ongolobɛ* is simply an ancestor spirit and that creation is an incomprehensible riddle, are at least 60 years old and thus were already adults when Christian theology began to filter into the area from the missions in the late 1920s or early 1930s. In addition, two men—both somewhere between 55 and 60 years old—independently and spontaneously recalled *Ongolobɛ* always being talked about as though he were an ancestor spirit in their youth but recognized that now many people look upon him differently. From these indications it would thus seem that the notion of *Ongolobɛ* as a timeless creator is a rather recent introduction. On the other hand, Kootz-Kretschmer reports the belief in *Ongolobɛ* as creator in the early twentieth century (1926: I, 234–5). However, since she was a missionary and her informant a convert, we are inclined to question this report.

shout obscenities: '*Olumɛ ampɛlɛ enfyubi* (Let a man give me a penis)!' and '*Ampɛlɛ empundɔ* (Give me a vagina)!' Since terms for sexual organs may normally be spoken only in the presence of peers of the same generation and then only for good reason, this behaviour clearly sets the occasion of an ancestor rite off as something special. Dancing and shouting often continue throughout the rites but in a less vigorous manner.

The prayers themselves begin with a rousing invocation in which the chief officiant calls upon the ancestors, some by name, to come and drink beer with their kinsmen. As each name is called out, the assistant officiant pours beer into the holes which were prepared previously (Plate IVa).

Hey you people! Wake up in your home, if you are there. Hey, Ndele, drink this beer! You people, if you are here in this compound, take this beer. Mlangali, drink this beer at your compound. Nkalanga, beer! Mwagamba, you, too, if you are here. You who are in the White Place [the realm of the ancestor spirits], we here in your compound are disappearing because of disease. We have come here, you people![3]

After the invocation the head of a white fowl is submerged in the beer now contained in the right-hand hole. The bird is held there until it drowns, its death signifying that the ancestors have answered the call of their children and are partaking of the ritual meal. Several tail feathers of the bird are then placed at the far edge of the *eshipɔnyɔ* for the ancestor spirits and the rest of the fowl plucked and roasted for the celebrants. (Plate IVb).

The major issues which have prompted the ceremony are then raised with the ancestors' spirits. Interspersed with the arguments, discussions, exhortations to the living, etc., which comprise the contents of the prayers, are additional invitations to the ancestor spirits to come and partake of the beer. Each time they are invited, more beer is poured for them. At some point in the ceremony the *abalyapayɔ* as a group are also called upon to drink.

Lineage members give the head officiant messages to relate to the ancestors, for only he has the right to address them directly. Occasionally he may delegate this power temporarily, however, and call upon someone else to speak. When all kinsmen have had their say, the

---

[3] This invocation is typical and comes from an ancestor rite held on the advice of a diviner to appease an ancestor believed to be preventing a wife of the lineage from conceiving.

speaker tells the ancestors that there are no other matters to discuss and bids them farewell.

As soon as the prayers are finished, kinsmen press forward to take the meat from the *eshipɔnyɔ* and drink the beer from the holes. The whole rite is a meal which the living share with the ancestral spirits.

Empongo, *the Ancestor Spirits, and Deviant Behaviour*

With this brief outline of the procedure of ancestor rites, we can now begin to examine the verbal content of these rites for information on the conceptualization of *empongo* and its relationship to social control. The data for this analysis come from two sources: (1) tape recordings of three ancestor ceremonies, and (2) notes on five other such ceremonies which we witnessed. The three verbatim texts represent *emputɔ* that were each convened for a different purpose. One rite was celebrated at the grave of the wife of the first settler of Ipepete during the annual ceremonies for the ancestors of the headman. The second was part of the funeral ceremonies for a headman, and the third was prompted by illness among several members of a commoner lineage. In quoting passages from these three ceremonies, we shall henceforth refer to them as Ceremony 1, 2, and 3 respectively.

Empongo is one of the primary themes of the ancestor rites. It is discussed not only in those rites specifically prompted by illness but in every other prayer addressed to the ancestors as well. Indeed the phrase '*Tiputa empongo* (We are praying about *empongo*)' is part of the opening formula for any words directed to the ancestors.

The following quotation exemplifies the importance of *empongo* in any kind of prayer directed to the ancestors. It comes from a meeting of headmen convened in the sacred grove in order to 'forbid' the rains which had begun unseasonally early. This meeting nevertheless allotted considerable time to questioning and berating the ancestors about diseases in the community. The manner in which this was done is typical of all discussions of disease which the writer observed during ancestor rites.

(I) Magɛndɔ [an ancestor], we pray about *empongo* which have begun again. The compound here has deteriorated. This place has had a change of heart [*-sangush-*]. Magɛndɔ, we pray about disease of the stomach, coughing, death! You [plural], stop them! Little children are vomiting. How have we erred [*-tul-*]? In what way have we spoiled [*-nandy-*] things? The country has gathered; it says, 'This place has changed!' The women are starting to walk alone: they stop having babies. . . . The country has great hardships. Day after day, keening! How have we erred [-*tul*-]? What have we done wrong [-*tul*-]? For what reason are there tears so often? You do not stop it, you people [the ancestors]. You, too, used to speak like this. Whose home is this? *It is yours!*

This passage reveals several significant things about the moral implications of disease and death. First, children die, illness is rampant, and women are barren because people have 'erred' (-*tul*-) or 'spoiled' (-*nandy*-) things. In other words, human action of some kind causes *empongo*. Second, it is the ancestors' job to reveal the manner in which people have erred and thereby stop the decimating effects of the *empongo*. This quotation thus implies a systematic relationship among the elements: *empongo*, human action, and the ancestors. In order to understand the nature of this relationship further, we must first comprehend what kind of human action is conceived as causing *empongo*. To do this, we shall examine the meanings of the terms -*nandy*- and -*tul*- more closely. Found repeatedly in the foregoing passage, these key words occur in ancestor rites time and again in relation to *empongo*.

The text of Ceremony 2 provides particularly good data on these concepts. This ceremony, it will be remembered, was held to welcome a former headman (Nkɛbeŋa) to the realm of the ancestor spirits. Mwadala, the son of the headman, had long been involved in a dispute with his father-in-law. One of Mwadala's children had been sick at the time of Nkɛbeŋa's funeral, and the new headman had been instructed to see that the relatives consulted a diviner to determine the cause. The diviner was never consulted, however.[4] This fact, plus the old, unsettled dispute had 'spoiled' the community, according to the principal speaker at the rites. In the course of his oration, this speaker described the activities in the community which had spoiled it and the contrasting situation towards which he wanted the community to move. It is this clear contrast made in the oration between the 'spoiled' and the 'repaired' community that makes Ceremony 2 particularly valuable in understanding the meanings of -*nandy*- and -*tul*-.

To orient the reader to the personnel involved in this ceremony, Figure 3 shows the reputed genealogical relationship among the persons mentioned in the following quotations. Because accurate genealogies are kept only to the grandparental generation, the number of links between Nkɛbeŋa and Mpɔnzi or between Mpɔnzi and the

[4] Additional details of this dispute may be found in Chapter IV, Case VII.

Disease, Death, Deviance, and the Ancestors

speaker, for example, may be apocryphal. It is for this reason that we have used the word 'reputed' to describe the genealogy. In other words, the genealogy represents sociological not biological fact.

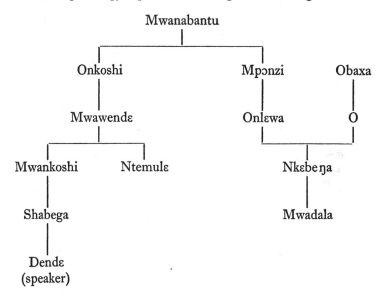

Figure 3—Reputed genealogical relationships of individuals mentioned in quotations from Ceremony 2.

An Analysis of the Term -nandy-
Using passages from Ceremony 2, we shall now examine the meaning of -*nandy*- from two perspectives: (1) from that of the contrast drawn in the prayers between the characteristics of 'spoiled' and 'unspoiled' social units; and (2) from the perspective of the terms used and the concepts involved in returning a spoiled social unit to its former state. (In the latter analysis we shall supplement the material from Ceremony 2 with quotations from other rites.)

1. *The Contrast between 'Spoiled' and 'Unspoiled' Social Units.*—In essence a social unit which has been spoiled is one in which the members act independently and do not consult one another about their activities. They may keep secrets from one another or talk 'carelessly' about one another.

(II) There are many children in the house of Mpɔnzi. Mpɔnzi, they want your house to come to an end. They are scattered about.... Let these children meet together and never quarrel again. . . . What is wrong with the children of this house? One steals from the other. Why do they spoil [-*nandy*-] the house?

Why does each child go about his business alone? They should try together; they should pray to the ancestors together. If the headmen say 'Are things well with you?', they should not just smile foolishly. They ask outsiders about this difficulty. Is this right?

They tell falsehoods about one another. Don't repeat wrong information about others—it is not good.

Failure to co-operate in consulting a diviner also indicates spoilage of the social unit.

(III) [addressed to the present headman, Nkɛbeŋa's successor] You who are facing me, why don't you go to consult a diviner? I am asking you, did you find out whether they [the other members of his lineage] had seen a diviner? If they left you alone to do this, did you ask them why they did so? The task of seeing a diviner requires co-operation. If you are alone, you can't do anything. Indeed, this compound is spoiled!

The concluding remarks of the ceremony summarize the qualities of a spoiled compound:

(IV) You there, Obaxa, their wife's father, tell Nkɛbeŋa that his children are not on good terms. Each one goes his own way. May he gather them together. Nkɛbeŋa, you yourself keep an eye on whoever speaks in an uncalled-for manner. You, too, Nkɛbeŋa, do not speak needlessly. Nkɛbeŋa, you have a case to settle. Collect your children. Do not be angry. Be friends, Nkɛbeŋa. Your children should be as you are with the other ancestor spirits.

This, then, is the picture of a compound which has been spoiled: the members go their own way, speak untruths about one another, steal from one another, are not concerned when their fellows are ill, and leave cases unsettled. In contrast with this condition are relations among the ancestor spirits, as the final statement in the preceding quotation suggests.

To see what this contrasting situation is like, let us observe the kind of welcome which Nkɛbeŋa's descendants envisage for him in the realm of the ancestor spirits.

(V) Receive Mpɔnzi[5] and offer him a chair. Welcome him and make him happy. You should not be thinking of things [wrongs] from the past. . . .

[5] Nkɛbeŋa is here referred to by his lineage name, i.e. by the name of the founder of the branch of the lineage which is segmentally opposite to that of the speaker.

Disease, Death, Deviance, and the Ancestors

Take this beer, you people. We intend to introduce this person[Nkɛbeŋa] to you today.... Receive your kinsman. Shake hands with him. Meet him and be together like those children who built compounds together in the past. They did not quarrel....

Gather amicably with Ntemulɛ; meet this kinsman of yours. Ntemulɛ, Mpɔnzi arrived yesterday; live well together. Nyesa, the newcomer who arrives today, be kind to him. Let him see his children. Introduce him to the others and receive him well. Onlɛwa, you left Mpɔnzi here in this compound. Help him repair [-*lengany*-] his compound.

This passage clearly portrays an unspoiled compound as one in which people are hospitable, courteous, do not harbour grudges, and do not quarrel—in short, where people live in unity and friendship. This notion is vividly summarized in the statement frequently made at ancestor rites: 'We should be of one heart [intention]' (*Tibɛ omwɔyɔ gumɔ*).

2. *Returning a 'Spoiled' Social Unit to its Former State.*—To achieve a deeper appreciation of the meaning of -*nandy*-, we shall now examine the manner in which a social unit may be retrieved from a discordant, spoiled state.

(VI) [the speaker addressing the headman of the community] Now, then, go and talk to one another. We have failed with you people. You yourselves talk it over. After you have discussed things together, brew beer. We shall all come to drink it and dance here.... Discuss this matter, you people. It is already very late. Don't refuse. Let us finish this matter.

Thus, through discussion will hopefully come unity of purpose, expressed in eating and dancing. The term used for this process of returning a social unit to a harmonious state (-*lengany*-) is also used with reference to objects, in the sense of making or fashioning something out of many parts or of mending or repairing something which has broken. The sense of the word is thus to create a whole or a unity out of disparate or temporarily separated parts.[6]

In conclusion, then, the term -*nandy*- refers to the activity of fragmenting a unit into disparate parts. A 'spoiled' social unit is thus one devoid of unity, where people pursue their own ends instead of the ends of the whole. In transitive forms the verb means to spoil by breaking into pieces. It is consistent with this analysis, moreover, that -*nandy*- is used only with reference to incorporative social relations—

[6] For the use of the term -*lengany*- in context, see quotation V above.

42 *Witchcraft, Sorcery, and Social Categories Among the Safwa*

i.e., to relations symbolized in a patrilineal idiom—where both unity and harmony are stressed.

An Analysis of the Term -tul-
In contexts where the personal referents and their relationship are ambiguous, -*nandy*- and -*tul*- are virtually synonymous. Thus, both terms may be used with the word *enɔŋgwa* to indicate the act of committing a wrong against another person, so long as the social relationship between the wrongdoer and the victim is unknown. For example: (*Atulilɛ* or *anandyilɛ*) *enɔŋgwa pahwibilɛ engɔmbɛ ezyaMwadala* (He committed a wrong when he stole Mwadala's cattle). In this sentence, if the relationship between the subject and Mwadala is incorporative, -*nandy*- should be used. If the relationship between the two is something else, then -*tul*- should be used.

The following quotation from a prayer to the ancestors provided us with a substitution frame for testing the contrast between these two terms in the field.

[Your] child here claims that the thing which fell up there [i.e. a lightning bolt which struck a house in the mountains] broke down the house! It just missed killing people! How has he erred [-*tul*-]? Indeed, if he has caused things to be disrupted [-*nangany*- from -*nandy*-] let an omen come. Tell us that our kinsman has spoiled [-*nandy*-] matters.

According to informants, the substitution of -*nandy*- for -*tul*- in the above passage would change the emphasis. As it stands, the speaker seems to suspect the kinsman of having disrupted a relationship with fellow kinsmen; with the terms substituted, it would seem that he suspects him more of disrupting a non-kin relationship. Although informants thus accepted the quotation with the two terms reversed, they felt that the above version was stronger, angrier—a likely response considering the implication of the statements.

The use of the term -*tul*- in other contexts, reveals an interesting connotation of the term. Thus, while -*nandy*- also refers to destroying or shattering things, -*tul*- extends to the domain of cooking. -*Tul*- means to make a fleshy plant food, such as potatoes or pumpkins, water-logged and tasteless through improper cooking. For example, the sweet potatoes (*amadulɛ*) in the sentence, *atulilɛ amadulɛ*, are mushy and insipid.

When we consider the previously mentioned association between heat and *inzyongoni* in Safwa thought, the use of the term -*tul*- in the contexts of both cooking or heating food and social relations becomes somewhat more intelligible. It would seem that whereas *-nandy-* implies an activity which completely dissociates an object or relationship, *-tul-* implies an activity which weakens the essential character (*inzyongoni*) of a food or a social relationship to the point of insipidity. This difference in connotation (signification?) accounts for the possibility of using the latter, but not the former, term with respect to transactional relations, which, as we have seen, cannot be shattered since they were never conceived as a unity.

In summary, *-nandy-* and *-tul-*, as used in the contexts cited above, constitute a category of behaviour in Safwa life, the distinguishing feature of which is the pursuit of one's private goals to the point of either breaking or weakening social relationships. To facilitate further discussion of these terms we shall categorize them under the rubric 'deviant behaviour'. In doing this we have shifted from Safwa folk categories to a Western analytic category. Nevertheless, we think the meaning of the two sets of categories is sufficiently close to warrant doing this.

The Relationship between Deviant Behaviour and Empongo

We have now established on the one hand that both *-nandy-* and *-tul-* are human actions that disrupt social relationships, either by fragmenting them or weakening them. On the other hand, we have concluded that *empongo* refers to the withdrawal or debilitation of the essential force (*inzyongoni*) of the individual. We shall now explore the relationship between these two concepts in some detail.

To do this, we return again to the text of Ancestor Ceremony 2. The main concern of this ceremony, it will be remembered, was a dispute between Mwadala and his father-in-law Onlaga. For a long time these two had been in disagreement, and this disagreement had led Mwadala to seek a divorce from Onlaga's daughter. On numerous occasions when Mwadala's children had been ill, Onlaga had refused to accompany him to a diviner to determine the cause of the illness. At the time of this ceremony another of Mwadala's children was sick and had been so for some time. The elders had previously instructed the disputants to consult a diviner together about this case but without effect. In his effort to persuade them once again to consult a diviner, the speaker in this rite revealed the relationship which Safwa see between *empongo* and disturbed social relationships.

Thus, at one point in the ceremony the speaker asked rhetorically,

'Why are there afflictions of the stomach and coughing here [i.e. in this community]?' His answer followed immediately: 'Each child [of the particular ancestors addressed] talks only with himself.' Or later when the protagonists discussed previous divinations for Mwadala's children and he was then asked why he had not consulted a diviner about the recent illness of one of his children, Mwadala reported, 'I *have* asked about it. He [the diviner] said, my friends, that this compound goes every which-way [i.e. the members do not act as a unit].'

Thus, in both these passages activities which fall under the category *-nandy-* are cited as causing *empongo*. Later in the ceremony, moreover, this activity is explicitly mentioned as causal. When the speaker, Ntosa by name, continued pressing Mwadala about his not going to a diviner for his son's illness, someone in the assemblage of elders interjected, 'Listen, Ntosa, you are talking about that person [Mwadala]. That child is not causing things to be disrupted [*-nangany-* from *-nandy-*]. Onlaga is! Onlaga has a terrible temper'. Thus the action of *-nandy-*, of pursuing one's private ends to the detriment of the group, was believed to be behind the child's illness.

In short, then, in the Safwa view the relationship between *-nandy-* or *-tul-*, on the one hand, and *empongo* on the other, is one of causality: deviant behaviour brings about the withdrawal of life force from individuals.

Empongo *and the Role of the Ancestor Spirits*

Ancestor Spirits as Bearers of Truth.—In the cause-effect relationship between deviant behaviour and *empongo*, the ancestor spirits are conceived as playing a major role by providing their descendants with information on the deviance which underlies cases of *empongo* within their common social unit. Thus the ancestor spirits of a particular lineage are seen as responsible for enlightening their offspring about the causes of *empongo* within the lineage, while the ancestors of the headman of a community are responsible for informing him of the source of *empongo* not only within the chiefly lineage but within the community as well. This information which the ancestors give is known as *oganga*, and we shall translate this term as 'diagnosis', although it has the connotation of 'remedy' or even 'oracle' as well.

This diagnostic function of the ancestors comes out clearly in the following quotation from Ceremony 3.

Omwanlima, Mwaniboŋu, help us with this diagnosis. Magɛndɔ, we are unable to make this diagnosis. There is nothing wrong with us; we walk together. May we understand why we cannot accomplish this task. The person who wants to consume us should be found out. If any of us has become an owl-man, let him be known. We want to catch him, so that he stops. The person who disrupts things [literally, turns things around] should be revealed by the diviners.

As suggested in the foregoing passage, the ancestor spirits reveal their diagnosis through diviners (*aganga*; singular *oŋganga*), who, as the etymology indicates, are literally diagnosticians. (*Oŋganga* consists of the personal class prefix plus the root, *-ganga*, which also appears in *oganga* with an abstract class prefix.) In addition, the ancestors may disclose their diagnoses through a dream, and people in Mwanabantu tribe frequently act in terms of interpretations given to dreams.

The ancestors of headmen, however, have a special method of revealing their diagnoses: by visiting special clairvoyants and informing them of a disturbed situation and its underlying causes. These clairvoyants—who are called *akuba* (singular, *onkuba*) or in ritual contexts *embela* (singular, the same form), literally 'jackals'—are otherwise normal, old people who are believed to have this special ability of seeing chiefly ancestor spirits.[7]

The following passage, which comes from a meeting of headmen in the sacred grove, illustrates the role of 'jackal' in informing people about deviant behaviour.

This thing which falls from above tears the house apart. It has force. How have we erred [*-tul-*]? We have not erred in anything. If we have spoiled [*-nandy-*] things, our kinsmen, let the jackal come. Let it show us the right way [*-langnyizy-*, from *-lengany-*; see p. 41 above].

Thus the ancestors, by informing their descendants of the underlying relation between a case of *empongo* and socially disruptive behaviour, play a very important role in the social system. This is not the ancestors' only involvement with *empongo*, however.

Ancestor Spirits as Bearers of empongo.—Since ancestor spirits are considered part of the lineage or community, a spoiled relationship with them may cause *empongo*, just as a disrupted relationship with a living person may do so. Thus an ancestor, who for some reason has

---

[7] Of the four *akuba* we knew in the area of Magombɛ, three were women. Moreover all of them had at some time lived in the compound of a headman—as sister, wife, or remote kinsman—and thus knew something of the politics of headmanship.

been angered over his descendants' behaviour, may cause *empongo* within the lineage.

For the most part, however, ancestors are seen as causing *empongo* by their failure to live up to their responsibility of informing their descendants of the reasons behind a particular case of *empongo*. It is believed that this failure permits those who are spoiling the social unit to persist in their activities and thereby increase the drain of vital force from members of the unit. Thus the speaker in the following passage, after having appealed to his forebears numerous times on earlier occasions, accuses them of causing *empongo*.

You bring *empongo*! You bring annihilation! Why, Mpoli? Why, Omwanlima? Why, Mwaniboŋu? Why, Magɛndɔ?

Ndɛlɛya, take this beer and eat together with your daughters. We, your kinsmen beseech you to listen to us. Now you people, you Mpoli and you Omwanlima, listen to us. . . . Please don't forget us. Why is this disease in our compound? You have spoiled [-*nandy*-] the compound!

Later in the same ceremony another ancestor is accused:

Mwansindɛ, why have you spoiled [-*nandy*-] this compound? You have brought *empongo* to this compound. Why is this? You have annihilated this compound with afflictions of the stomach.

Thus, by failing to fulfil their role within the lineage, the ancestors, like the living, may inflict *empongo* on its members.

SUMMARY AND CONCLUSIONS

We have now outlined the relationship between three concepts: *empongo*, the ancestor spirits, and a category of human activity which we have translated as 'deviance'. This activity which, as we have seen, involves pursuing one's own ends to the point of disrupting an incorporative social relationship or weakening a transactional one, is believed to cause *empongo*, the withdrawal of vital force. In this event the ancestors are expected to inform members of the debilitated social unit about the behaviour which is causing *empongo*. This they do through diviners, dreams, and—in the case of headmen—clairvoyants.

The ideological structure here consists of three parts: (1) the essential state of an individual, (2) the condition of social conformity within a group—these two conceived as causally related, and (3) a group of entities capable of perceiving the relationship between

IIIA Paraphernalia ready for an ancestor ceremony: pots and gourds of beer, white cocks, trays of millet flour, and a butchered calf (*rear*). The grave is marked by the tree trunk (*centre*)

B Food distribution at ancestor rites. An officiant is cutting pieces of meat for distribution to key kinsmen of the deceased. This is done before the prayers are begun

IVa The *eshiponyo*. The officiant pours beer into one of the two holes which have been dug for the dead. Millet flour and meat have already been placed around the holes

b Cock being offered to the ancestors. The head of the fowl is being held in the beer which has been poured for the ancestors

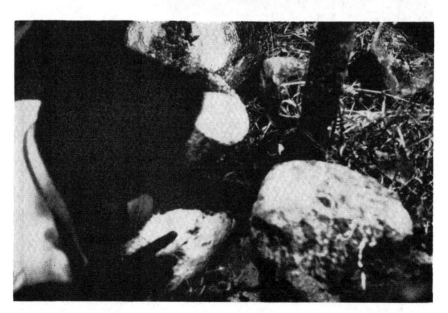

Disease, Death, Deviance, and the Ancestors 47

specific (1)'s and (2)'s. Presented in this perspective, the temporal relationship between parts (1) and (2) is: a change in (2) leads to a change in (1). In actual life, however, this temporal chain is reversed. A Safwa speaker observes the state of an individual first and from that, through the help of a diviner or the ancestors, comes to learn about the underlying social cause. In reality *empongo* serves as an indicator of deviance in social relationships.

This conclusion leads us to a second and complementary observation about the system of ideas we have outlined. The system expresses in its own way an important fact about human behaviour: namely, that the individual personality (self) is directly dependent both in its origin and continued expression on a 'social environment; . . . an organized set or pattern of social relations and interactions' (Mead 1964:242–3). When the accepted pattern of social interactions breaks down, the self suffers. In Safwa terms the self, symbolized by the *inzyongoni*, becomes weakened (i.e. *empongo* sets in) when others deviate from the 'organized set' of social relations.

An important implication of this view is that deviations in different kinds of social relationships may be conceived as causing different kinds of *empongo*—that is, the classification of the causes of *empongo* parallels the classification of social relationships. To examine this implication, we shall analyse the aetiology of *empongo* in the following two chapters.

CHAPTER III

SAFWA AETIOLOGICAL CATEGORIES

The last chapter concluded by pointing out that the cause-effect relationship posited in Safwa thought between disrupted social relations and the weakening of an individual's life force (i.e., *empongo*) logically implies a classification of the causes of *empongo* which parallels the classification of social relationships. The following two chapters examine this observation by analysing the various terms in the aetiology of *empongo*.

Because cases of *empongo* are diagnosed through either divination or autopsy, these activities provide natural scenes for eliciting the universe of aetiological terms in the Safwa dialect and will therefore supply the raw material for our analysis of beliefs about the causes of *empongo*. Consequently the first part of this chapter is devoted to an account of the routines, paraphernalia, and settings for both divination and autopsy. Afterwards we shall consider the range of terms which are appropriate in these diagnostic settings for describing the causes of *empongo*. Our aim is to arrive at the universe of terms used for this purpose.

After thus isolating this universe of terms and discussing beliefs surrounding them, in the following chapter we shall examine how these terms are applied in concrete instances. We shall do this by reference to actual cases of *empongo* recorded in the field.

DIVINATION AND AUTOPSY: THE BACKGROUND

Divination
Personnel.—Divining (*alagulɛ*; -*lagul*-, 'divine') is performed by certain specialists known as *aganga abalagulɛ* (singular *oŋganga owɛlagulɛ*). These specialists are distinguished from *aganga abɛmazizi* (from *onzizi*, 'medicine'), who specialize in preparing curative substances and do not possess the requisite power to divine. This power is known as *itonga*, a term which we shall consider more fully below and simply define for the present as the power to understand and perform hidden things (*evintu byahuwelu*, 'things in the dark').

In addition to their divining activities, *aganga abalagulɛ* specialize in medicines to combat attacks by people with *itonga* and may also prepare maleficent medicines. Although they may know how to prepare curative medicines as well, these practitioners frequently send their clients to one of the *aganga abɛmazizi* for treatment, if the condition which has been diagnosed is not caused by *itonga*. The *aganga abɛmazizi* never treat a case concerning *itonga*.

Thus *aganga abalagulɛ* are clearly distinguished from *aganga abɛmazizi* in Safwa practice not only by their ability to divine through the power of *itonga* but also by their unique ability to treat cases pertaining to *itonga*. For clarity of expression in English, we shall in future translate *oŋganga owɛlagulɛ* as 'diviner' and *oŋganga owɛmazizi* as 'medicine man'. We have already discussed the construction and meaning of the word *oŋganga* in the previous chapter (pp. 44-5).

Diviners vary in reputation, and on the whole those living at a distance are rated as being more powerful than those nearby. At the time I was in the field there were roughly four ranks of diviners from the vantage point of residents of Ipepete. The highest rank was occupied by Chikanga, a Malawian whose renown drew clients from all over south-western Tanzania, eastern Zambia and Malawi. Next was a supposed disciple of the great Chikanga, who assumed the name of his mentor and lived in Itimba, the largest centre of population in the region. Next in repute were a number of diviners seen around Safwa territory at no less than ten miles from Ipepete, and last were Mlɔzi (a man of the neighbouring community) and a few diviners elsewhere whose powers were frequently questioned.

Only the great Chikanga and possibly his namesake were full-time specialists. There were no Safwa *aganga* who did not also cultivate their own fields.

Consultation of a Diviner.—The following circumstances lead Safwa to consult a diviner.

1. *Empongo.*—Although *empongo* is a standard answer to the question 'Why do you go to a diviner (*Mulagula pali weli*)?' not all cases of *empongo* are actually submitted to divination. If the victim or his kinsmen can identify the disease themselves, the divination is omitted and the case brought directly to a medicine man. Only if people do not know or understand (-*meny*-) the disease is a diviner consulted. Safwa do not 'understand' a disease under the following circumstances: (a) when the symptoms appear very suddenly, (b) when the illness lingers for an

unusually long time, (c) when the victim is severely incapacitated, or (d) if they have received no diagnosis from the ancestor spirits through dreams. Certain symptoms—stabbing pains, vomiting of blood—are immediately understood as evidence of a personal attack through the power of *itonga*. These cases are promptly taken to a diviner.
2. Some but not all thefts.
3. Diseases and death of cattle.
4. 'Gardens', i.e. poor harvests.
5. 'If women do not bear children.' This includes both failure to conceive and difficulty in giving birth.
6. Destruction of a house or other property by lightning.

This list was compiled from case histories which the writer collected in and around Ipepete and from answers to the direct question, 'Why do you go to a diviner?' The information appears in the order of frequency with which the enumerated causes actually led to a divination in a record of consultations kept at the ethnographer's request by two diviners, who were paid for their services. The diviners' records include data on their clients' places of residence, on the immediate problems which evoked each divination, the diagnosis, and any subsequent activity arising from the diagnosis.

The records were kept independently by each diviner for one week's time in the months of June and October 1963 and February 1964.[1] These months were chosen because they mark varied events in the local seasonal and agricultural cycles. Thus June is a dry-season month in which the main millet crop is harvested, October occurs at the end of the dry season and is a month in which fields are prepared for planting, and February falls well into the rainy season at a time when short food supplies are just being augmented by early maize. Table I presents a tabulation of the diviners' records with respect to the problems which occasioned the divinations they performed.

Although the total number of cases is relatively small (41), it does constitute a complete record of divinations sought from two diviners over a set period of time and thus gives some indication of the relative frequency with which divinations result from various causes.

[1] One of the diviners was literate in Swahili and kept his own records in that language. The records of the other diviner were kept by a young kinsman who lived with him.

TABLE I

FREQUENCY OF DIVINATIONS AND THEIR IMMEDIATE CAUSES

	Diviner A June Oct. Feb. (one-week periods)	Diviner B June Oct. Feb. (one-week periods)	Totals
empongo	3 2 5	3 4 5	22
theft	1 1 1	1 0 2	6
illness or death of cattle	0 1 1	1 2 0	5
gardens	2 0 1	1 0 1	5
barrenness	0 0 1	0 1 0	2
difficulty in childbirth	0 0 0	0 0 1	1
	6 4 9	6 7 9	41

There is little correspondence between the frequency of consultation for the various reasons mentioned in Table II and people's evaluations of the importance of these different reasons. Thus despite the high frequency with which people consulted the diviners about theft, this event is evaluated as a much less important cause for seeking a divination than cattle diseases, gardens or difficulty in childbirth, while this last item is evaluated second only to *empongo* in importance.

When the occasion for a divination arises, certain people are called upon to participate in the actual consultation. To a large extent each occasion defines those who participate. Table II lists those most likely to seek a divination, given the precipitating situation. In general they may be seen to include members of the victim's families of orientation and procreation.

A prospective client is usually referred to a diviner by a friend, unless he already has a close association with one. Often the friend who arranges for a divination accompanies the clients to the diviner's house; or in situations of *empongo* or complications in childbirth, when the victim is too incapacitated to be moved, he may guide the diviner to where the victim is staying.

Although the go-between is a standard Safwa mode of approaching those with whom one seeks a transactional relationship, as we have seen, in this case the go-between also functions to inform the diviner of some of the details of the local scene. Informants who had served as go-betweens claimed that the diviner never asks specific questions about the case but just talks generally. (*Tiyaŋanayaŋa hashɛ*—'We just talk to one another a bit'.) I was not able to determine how much information about the case the go-between actually supplies, and undoubtedly this varies a great deal with the diviner's prior knowledge of the community in question and his relationship with the go-between.

TABLE II

CLIENTS SEEKING INITIAL DIVINATIONS FOR VARIOUS PRECIPITATING SITUATIONS

Situation	Clients
empongo	
victim-adult male	father and/or brother, adult sons
victim-adult unmarried female	father and/or brothers,[a] a representative of intended husband's lineage (if applicable)
victim-adult married female	husband, husband's father or brother, kinsman of woman (father or brother[a])
victim-widow	sons
theft	person robbed[b]
difficulty in childbearing	woman, husband, woman's father or brother[a]
illness or death of cattle	owner or owners
gardens	cultivator[b]

[a] Full siblings only.
[b] A woman, however, consults a diviner only with her husband or lineal male kinsman.

If clients are not satisfied with the results of a first divination, they may seek another either from a different *oŋganga* or even from the same one. Fees for divination vary widely, depending on the reputation of the diviner, the clients' relationship with him, and the nature of the case. The lowest fee the writer recorded (one shilling) was for a case of theft, divined by a man of no special reputation for a close friend of his son-in-law. The highest fee, paid to the Malawian Chikanga, was 200 shillings for a case brought by an entire community against a man reputedly stealing milk from cows by supernatural means.

Paraphernalia and Techniques of Divination.—Since a detailed description of the paraphernalia and techniques of divination is not

Safwa Aetiological Categories

directly relevant to the present analysis, only a brief outline will be included. The purpose of this brief account, however, is to provide specific data from which a general statement about divinatory procedures can be made.

The major techniques used in divination today include:

1. A talking gourd, operated by the diviner, which asks questions of clients and makes diagnoses on the basis of their responses;
2. a coin which the diviner stands on edge and stares at before asking the clients leading questions which are thought to be prompted in some way by the coin;
3. diviner and clients frame questions that are answered by the diviner on the basis of the way the hairs of a civet skin fall after being blown upon;
4. the diviner uses a glass stopper from a decanter as a crystal ball and determines the problem and solutions by peering into the ball and asking clients questions suggested by images 'seen' there;
5. certain antelope horns, filled with 'medicine', detect those who have *itonga* by 'flying' in their direction;
6. the diviner throws down beads and 'reads' the answers to questions from the patterns in which the beads fall;
7. certain diseases caused by *itonga* are detected by smelling the victim.

Fashions in divination change, however, and Kootz-Kretschmer (1926) describes other methods prevalent at the beginning of the century.

1. A 'chair oracle' which shakes or stands still in response to questions addressed it (I, 258–60);
2. an animal's horn, filled with medicines, which answers questions put to it by the client and ventriloquist-diviner (I, 257–8);
3. various roots whose knotty exteriors are 'read' (I, 257);
4. stirring ashes with an axe; if the ashes stick, the answer is 'yes' to the question asked (I, 263).

Although the specific methods may differ, the basic format of these divinations is the same: a series of questions and answers between the diviner and client with an 'impartial' device which affirms or negates certain yes-no questions.

Certain diviners determine causes of death today by digging into the deceased's grave, usually about one month after burial. The diviner's verdict in such a case may be based on the amount of 'heat' in the grave, the placement of the corpse, and/or certain 'medicines' found with the body. (This is not a complete inventory of signs used in this type of divination; they are merely three which I observed.)

In general, then, the diviner knows at least something about the local or familial situation of his clients before the actual divination takes place. Moreover, as many of the preceding examples show, divining includes not only diagnostic and causal statements but also questions which involve clients in the process of producing an interpretation of the facts which rings true for them. Thus divination may be looked upon basically as a mutual process of interpreting facts, in which the divinatory apparatus—the gourd, the door, the coin, etc.—serves in successful instances to confirm a particular interpretation of the situation agreed upon by the clients and the diviner.

In Section II of this chapter and in the succeeding chapter we shall present data to show precisely which aspects of social and disease situations are relevant in arriving at an acceptable divinatory interpretation.

Autopsy
Before the British imposed a ban on autopsies under Native Authority legislation, post-mortem examinations were held after almost every Safwa death. Each community had an operator who performed its autopsies, and only members of the community and close kin of the deceased might be present beside the corpse when the operation was performed. If an outsider attempted to see the proceedings, he was driven away and ran the risk of being speared.

Although today each community still has its operator, autopsies are held much less regularly and never when any outsider associated with the Government is present. Other than this unvarying restriction, however, the writer was unable to discover exactly what circumstances determine when an autopsy *will* be performed today.

In operating, the following organs are examined specifically and may be removed either wholly or in part: the liver, gall bladder, spleen, stomach, and intestines. The presence or absence of blood in the abdominal cavity is also specifically noted. The examination is accompanied by a running discussion among the operators and spectators concerning the state of the organs and possible diagnoses.

The final verdict as to cause of death is always enunciated by the operator and the local headman, however.

THE CAUSES OF *EMPONGO*

In the previous section we outlined the basic data on both divination and autopsy, the two formal situations in Safwa life which elicit systematic selections among alternative causes of *empongo*. We shall now concentrate on the various causes themselves. The following sections treat these causes in terms of Safwa belief, rather than action. The information derives from discussions with informants about the various causes which the ethnographer heard given for actual cases of illness or death. The discussions were not necessarily limited to particular cases, however; rather, the cases served to initiate a general consideration of possible causes. The purpose of this section is to survey the linguistic array available to the Safwa for ascribing a cause to a particular instance of *empongo* and to provide an overview of Safwa thinking about these causes.

Following this exposition, we shall compare Safwa beliefs with those of other African societies. In the course of this comparison, we shall re-examine some traditional anthropological thinking about witchcraft and sorcery in the light of Safwa data.

Empongo *Diagnosed by Divination*

Empongo *caused by the Ancestors* (empongo ezyangolobɛ)
This category of *empongo* pertains to all *empongo* inflicted either by commoner ancestors on members of their own descent group or by chiefly ancestors on members of their community. Although in the previous chapter we have already discussed the role of the ancestors in causing *empongo*, there are nevertheless some remaining beliefs which need to be covered here.

The Safwa term for these *empongo* designates them as being 'of *Ongolobɛ*'. We have already spoken of the various conceptions of *Ongolobɛ*, the Supreme Being of Safwa cosmology. His association with these *empongo*, which are ascribed to the ancestors, corroborates the interpretation of this Being as the first ancestor rather than as Creator, since—as senior ancestor—he would naturally be held responsible for the actions of his juniors in bringing *empongo*. Despite this ultimate attribution of these *empongo* to *Ongolobɛ*, however, it is the ancestors themselves who actually deprive kinsmen of their life force. This they do for three reasons: loneliness, neglect of responsibility, or anger.

Ancestor spirits are thought to grow lonely for spouses who have long survived them and eventually come to take their *inzyongoni* to the White Place. It is generally claimed that many old people die in this fashion. In fact, however, for any particular case it would seem to depend on one's position in the social structure whether or not he actually accepts this interpretation of the cause of death. We shall take up this matter in greater detail in Chapter V, with reference to Case VI.

As we have noted in the previous chapter, one of the primary responsibilities of the ancestor spirits is to inform their descendants of the social disruption which is at the root of cases of *empongo*. If the spirits fail in this duty, the incidence of *empongo* is believed to increase, since their helpful guidance is needed to remove the underlying cause. In addition to providing diagnoses for active cases of *empongo*, the ancestor spirits are also conceived as protecting the *inzyongoni* of their descendants from attacks from outsiders. Because of this function, in a sense almost any *empongo* may be construed as due to their negligence. In fact, however, they are only blamed openly if they are believed to have failed in their duty to provide the proper diagnosis.

Anger, the third reason for the ancestor spirits' inflicting *empongo* on their descendants, was discussed in one of its aspects in the previous chapter. There we noted that an ancestor who is indignant over the behaviour of his descendants may bring *empongo* upon one of them. But ancestor spirits may be angry not only with the living but also with one another. Thus two forbears who argued in life and died without reconciling their differences may also cause *empongo* to strike within the descent group. These *empongo* are known generically as those which 'follow in a lineage' because they crop up generation after generation until the underlying dispute has either been settled or caused a split within the descent group. The three major *empongo* of this type are *ehatuli*, *empongo embibi*, and *eshitasi*. We shall describe the second and third of these briefly, but insufficient information prevents us from doing this for the first.

Empongo embibi.—Although this *empongo* is said to strike people of any age, the cases I observed were all in children. The patient is said to suffer from diarrhoea and weakness; in the terminal stages there is a lightening of the skin of the extremities, and the skin over the fontanel is said to become depressed. Although these symptoms occur frequently in association with fatalities in children, they are diagnosed as *empongo embibi* only in certain lineages. Indeed often the affliction is diagnosed without divination and is treated only by specialists in the illness.

In the past victims of this disease were not accorded proper burial but were simply thrown into the bush. Although today they are buried, the funerary procedure is unusual. The corpse is anointed with medicine and then interred with all his personal belongings. During the interment no keening is permitted, since to do so is believed to spread the disease within the lineage. Victims of *empongo embibi*, moreover, are never mentioned by name in prayers to the ancestors. Instead they are believed to be among 'those who eat separately' in the ancestor rites.

Eshitasi.—The outward symptoms of this *empongo* are said to parallel closely those of *empongo embibi*, and victims are buried in the same manner. One informant claimed that *eshitasi* might even turn into *empongo embibi*.

Itonga *as a cause of* empongo

In our previous discussion of diviners we introduced the term *itonga* and simply defined it there as 'the power to understand and perform "hidden things." ' It is now necessary to analyse this concept further.

When asked outright 'What is *itonga*?' (*Itonga lyɛnu?* or *Itonga lili wili?*), trusted informants invariably answered that it is doing things to others without being seen. One informant gave the very graphic example of having sexual relations with a sleeping woman without waking her. From this example and later discussion prompted by it, it would seem that *itonga* is an explanation of situations which one knows occurred (i.e. one accepts the fact—on whatever grounds—that the woman in the example did actually have sexual relations) but which one cannot explain by visible means. In other words *itonga* is the power to act, unperceived by others.

This defining characteristic of the term leads to its use in two ways. First, it may be used in a general sense to describe any situation in which the underlying interpersonal causes are not apparent. It is merely a way of expressing confusion over the precise causality of an event. The range of possible causes entertained by Safwa and by

Westerners are of course different, as our present discussion of the causes of disease will indicate; but whenever the cause is unknown, people may speak of *itonga*. The second use of the term derives both from the notion of invisible power and from the idea that in many cases diminutions of human power (*inzyongoni*) are humanly caused, a concept which we noted in the previous chapter. The logic of these two assumptions leads to the postulation that there are certain humans, the *abitonga* (singular, *omwitonga*), who possess the power to act invisibly and employ this power in interpersonal relations. In short, the term in the first sense refers to an attribute of a situation, while in the second sense it refers to an attribute of a person. These two senses fuse in situations when a diviner has ruled out all other possible causes and indicates that a person with *itonga* is responsible for bringing about a disease or a death.

The power of *itonga* may be inherited patrilineally by both males and females, but not all children need inherit. There is no physical manifestation of this power observable either externally or internally, although post-mortem evidence of the *empongo* called '*endasa*' indicates that the victim was engaged in a mutual battle of *itonga* and thus a possessor of the power himself. The activities which are inspired by *itonga* are carried out at night by the *inzyongoni* of the possessor of this power.

There are two kinds of *itonga*, good (*linza*) and bad (*libibi*). Good *itonga* is used for the benefit of a social unit, while bad *itonga* is used against it. One kind of *itonga* may be converted to the other so that a person, who has previously used his powers for the benefit of the community, may suddenly employ them to its detriment. Thus diviners—who, as we noted, possess the power of *itonga* and use it beneficially to diagnose the causes of disease—may sometimes be suspected of using it detrimentally, as the following passage from a prayer to the ancestors shows.

> The diviners are saying that there are many [people with bad *itonga*]. They should tell the truth! They say there are many—perhaps they know. They should not spread rumours about one another. They want just to acquire money from people. They should not acquire money from the body and blood of others!

Good *itonga* may be converted to bad *itonga* privately by the will of the possessor, but bad *itonga* may be changed to good only by drinking a 'medicine' prepared by a person with stronger powers or by public avowal of a change of heart. It is said that a person whose *itonga* has been converted from bad to good would die should he revert to his old, malevolent ways.

Thus *itonga* itself is a neutral power which can be used in either a moral or immoral fashion. As one informant described people with *itonga*, 'They are like keys, which can both open and close doors'. Employed in either a moral or immoral manner, however, *itonga* is always a matter of conscious intent and the user considered morally responsible.

Good itonga.—In addition to its use for divining, good *itonga* may be used to protect people without any *itonga* from the attacks of those who use their invisible powers in a malicious manner. Thus within every community there is said to be a league of elders who not only protect residents from attacks from without by means of *itonga* but may also punish their co-residents for unco-operative behaviour.

For example, a man who is disagreeable and refuses to settle or answer questions involving a case (a person, in short, who spoils, -*nandy*-, the community) may be made ill by the combined power of those with *itonga*. To use the power in this way is termed *agunɛ* and is not morally reprehensible behaviour.[2] The victim of such a combined attack is said to be afflicted with insomnia and general loss of strength (*ixonɛ*), but few victims are said to die from these attacks. It is relevant to note that neither of the two cases of *agunɛ* in our data fit this description, however. One concerns a swollen arm and the other a death. It would appear that the verbal description given expresses something about the debilitating effects of *empongo* in general rather than the specific symptoms which prompt a diagnosis of *agunɛ*.

Since employing one's *itonga* in this way to 'repair' the community is highly approved, some heads of households occasionally perform minor feats of divination in order to establish themselves publicly as men of good *itonga*. Frequently these demonstrations occur at

[2] The similarity between these beliefs and those of the neighbouring Nyakyusa concerning 'the defenders' (G. Wilson 1936:86–9; M. Wilson 1963:96–102) is too close to pass without mention. Although the Safwa do not speak in terms of 'the breath of man', the term *agunɛ* is cognate with the Nyakyusa noun *ikigunɛ*, which is used in both Ngonde and the Selya dialect of Nyakyusa and is translated by Wilson as 'the effect of "the breath of men" . . . "the curse" ' (1963:101). Nor do the Safwa have the python symbolism so important in Nyakyusa thought about 'defenders', although they do associate pythons with headmen and sacred groves. The two ideologies seem to be virtually identical, differing only in content at the specific points mentioned.

communal beer drinks and involve an accusation that someone present is drinking the beer by secret means. One informant recounted an incident in which he stooped over the beer pot in order to take a drink and claimed to have seen the level of the liquid fall before he even put his drinking straw into the pot. One of the elders present announced that someone had drunk the beer by means of mystical power (*itonga*). When he warned the person to stop, the beer level was supposed to have risen again. Whatever the empirical explanation of this supposed occurrence, it was believed true by many people and served to establish the elder as a man of good *itonga*.

Disputes between communities over boundaries or, in the past, women also involve people with good *itonga*, who are believed to launch attacks on the enemy at night, just as the warriors attack by day. In the late 1940s, for example, Isoko had a border dispute with the neighbouring settlement of Igala. The headmen of Igala and Isoko were from different segments of the same lineage. Although the dispute was fought by day in the Magistrate's Court, which ruled in favour of Isoko, the decisive battles for the Safwa took place at night. The court ruling was merely considered proof that the Isoko defenders had indeed routed the foe in their nocturnal forays.

Bad itonga.—There are two principal activities in which people with bad *itonga* engage: -*lody*- and -*ly*-. *Alodyɛ* is to introduce foreign substances (*amalila*; singular *ilila*) into another person's body or into his gardens to diminish their effectiveness. The substances used are most often said to be small bones, but stones or balls of hair or grass also serve. The substances are believed to enter the body of the victim when the possessor feels anger but does not express it. The victim of *alodyɛ* becomes ill and may die. Significantly, however, the symptoms associated with this condition are very general and do not include swelling or a local irritation caused by the foreign substance. The substance is symbolic of the unexpressed anger rather than an irritant itself and weakens the victim by pervading his system.

Alyɛ is best translated as 'to consume' and is used to express not only normal eating but also embezzlement and the activity of the *inzyongoni* of a person with bad *itonga*, when it goes by night to destroy or weaken its victim. A male *inzyongoni* is said to be accompanied by that of a female, who carries a winnowing tray in which the flesh of the victim is placed. It is believed that only if the meat is actually ingested by the *abitonga* does the victim die; otherwise he simply becomes feckless and ill. A death caused by being 'consumed' is recognized in post-mortem examination by the presence of lacerations and blood on the liver.

It should be noted, however, that just as the noun *itonga* may be used with either a specific or generic referent, so the verb *-ly-* may be used either in a general sense to describe any activity which is suspected of having been carried out by *abitonga* or in the specific sense described above. Thus a person may say, '*Balilɛ onu* (They have consumed that person)', when he does not know the precise nature of the illness but merely suspects bad *itonga*. Or he may mean quite specifically that a group of people have consumed someone's vitals. In future we shall use the term *-ly-* only in this more specific sense, unless otherwise stipulated.

Some people with bad *itonga* are believed to have the ability to change themselves into owls or hyenas when they go out stalking their victims. One distinguishes these owl- or hyena-men (*enkwitwa-muntu, enfisi-muntu*) from wild types by the fact that they prowl near a particular house night after night. These were-creatures are believed to consume (*-ly-*) their victims and may be apprehended only if hunted naked. Should such a beast be killed, the next day a person in the community will, it is said, be found dead—proof that he was the culprit.

People with bad *itonga* are also believed capable of two other activities. The first is to tie closed (*-tat-* or *-piny-*) the wombs of women in the community to prevent them from conceiving. It is said that these people similarly bind the intestines of men to prevent them from defecating, although we never encountered direct accusations to this effect. The final activity in which bad *abitonga* engage is perverting people's natures (*-galandy-*, from the root *-gal-*, 'turn'). A person who has been perverted in this way 'may just begin to consume [*-ly-*] people or to remain silent or insult people when previously he was polite' (informant's statement).

A person with *itonga* is believed capable of consuming (*-ly-*) only a member of his own lineage, although groups of people with bad *itonga* may combine forces and kill a non-relative. It is assumed that only by this accumulated strength of several *abitonga* may a non-kinsman be overcome. This practice, however, is said to lead to debts of 'hospitality' in which a person, who has called upon others to help him kill, becomes obligated to aid his accomplices in any killing they wish to do. Should a debtor refuse, he is reportedly 'speared' (*-las-*) by his associates. This cause of death is revealed at autopsy by the presence of blood in the abdominal cavity and will be discussed at greater length under cases diagnosed in this manner.

One can protect one's self from people with bad *itonga* not only by living among those with good *itonga* but also by procuring 'medicines' from a specialist. These medicines are designed to strengthen the body against attack and are rubbed directly into the blood through cuts made at strategic locations. These locations include the nape of the neck, the base of the throat, the chest, and the bases of the thumb and first toe. Other medicines, designed specifically to combat owl- or hyena-men, work through camouflage. They delude the malefactor into thinking that a swamp or pool is the house of the intended victim, and when the marauder goes to enter the house, he falls into the water and drowns. We shall have more to say about these medicines in the following section.

'Medicine' (onzizi) *as a cause of* empongo

Onzizi is a general term for substances which alter a vexing situation. It is usually made from plants, although the term may be extended to include oil for a bicycle, insecticide, or spirit for lighting pressure stoves. Its use was also recorded with reference to taxes as 'the medicine of the government (*onzizi gwasɛrikali*)' in a speech by the Chief to explain the workings of the central government. These examples are obviously all applications of the term to new situations but are nevertheless revealing of its root meaning.

Formal and functional classifications of medicines. In its unextended sense *onzizi* labels three different kinds of substances: *empenga*—dry, powdered medicine; *embɔzyɔ*—infusions made from the leaves of plants; and *onzizi*$_2$—infusions prepared from bark or roots. There are two contrast sets within this classification of medicines: one based on physical state and the other on ingredients. The taxonomy is displayed in Figure 4.[3]

Apart from this classification of medicines on the basis of form, Safwa also recognize a functional classification in which medicines are conceived as performing the following tasks (*imbɔmbɔ*): (1) enhancing already existing interpersonal relations or individual states; (2) repairing (-*lengany*-) a spoiled relation or state; or (3) degrading

[3]This taxonomy was derived from direct questioning of informants using examples of different types of medicines. The *significata* of the three classes and their relationships were inferred from informants' responses to questions, testing of alternative groupings by the investigator, and assignment of new examples to the correct class by the investigator.

or spoiling (*-nandy-*) a pre-existing favourable condition or situation.

There is no one-to-one correspondence between the functional classification of medicines and the previously mentioned formal one, since a particular medicine or class of medicines may work in more than one way. For example, certain specific substances which are designed to enhance the productivity of gardens also on occasion cause death within the community and thus degrade or spoil it. The formal class of this medicine does not alter but its functional role obviously does. To cite another example, certain medicines of the formal class *empenga* are used to strengthen a person's capacity to withstand attacks from those with *itonga*, while other substances of this same class are used to cause death. Thus no discrete assignment of individual medicines to functional classes is possible.

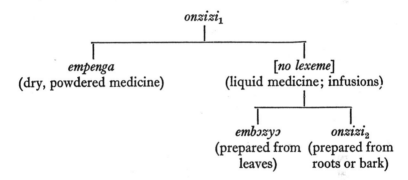

Figure 4—Taxonomy of *onzizi*₁

Since we are primarily concerned in this discussion with the effects of medicines in producing disease, the following treatment of this topic will therefore be organized around the functional rather than the formal classification of medicines.

Medicines for enhancing interpersonal relations or individual states. Medicines for strengthening human relationships are used at almost every level of group (incorporative) interaction. In the compound a special gourd (*enfinga*) is usually maintained by the compound head to strengthen his group against disease and malevolence from outside. In the community medicines are placed in the beer prepared twice a year for joint consumption, in order to prevent fighting and promote peaceful relations within the group. The community headman also maintains an *enfinga* from which warriors would formerly drink in order to give them strength in battle. Within the tribe there is a special medicine, *empampa*, which is eaten whenever local headmen come together in the major sacred grove. This medicine is designed to strengthen co-operation and peaceful relations among the tribal leaders. Thus all incorporative relationships are marked by the joint consumption of medicines.

Other medicines are believed to strengthen the state of the individual. *Ilulu*, for example, enhances the life force of people to protect them from the attacks of those with *itonga*. For the same reason certain kinds of powdered medicines are rubbed into cuts made at various locations on the body. Other medicines may be applied to the face to fortify one's ability to withstand attacks from jealous people or to make one appear more suitable to a prospective mate or employer. There are also medicines which elevate an individual or compound by increasing the yield from gardens or livestock.

Medicines which repair or restore a spoiled state. The most frequently used of these restorative medicines are for *empongo*. Numerous home remedies, as well as those procured from medicine men, serve to cure people of those *empongo* which are 'known' (*empongo ezyatimɛnyɛ*).

Many other restorative medicines return people to their normal conditions when they have been wrenched from it by such special events as the death of a child or spouse, by the birth of a child (particularly twins), or by having killed someone. The ceremonies which terminate these special states are known collectively as *embongɔ* and always include the drinking of medicine.

Restorative medicines are also used to return disequilibrated social relationships to parity. Thus indebtedness and theft of property belonging to a member of the same community mar relationships normally characterized by reciprocity, and there are medicines designed to re-equilibrate such relationships. Thus *amendombela* (also called *amapesu*) uncovers the identity of thieves by inducing them to confess their deeds publicly and offer restitution. We shall also discuss the role of the medicine *olupɛmbɛ* in effecting payment of unsettled debts below.

Medicines which degrade or spoil pre-existing situations. Medicines which are designed either to strengthen or restore situations may instead cause disease or degradation of relationships. We have already given an example of a medicine, procured to enhance the productivity of gardens, which instead begins to cause death within a lineage or community. This belief raises a very significant point about medicines. We have seen that medicines are widely used to enhance relationships within incorporative units. These medicines operate in this way, however, only if drunk or applied communally by every member of the unit. Thus we were informed after one lineage had convened to drink medicine in order to stop an *empongo*, that the medicine would not work because one member of the lineage had been absent from the rite. Thus medicines, if procured for purposes of enhancing a situation, must enhance everyone within the incorporative unit. This explains the example of the wayward medicine described above. The procurer of the medicine is believed to have obtained the substance not to enhance his whole community but to improve himself. This kind of action is undertaken at the expense of the community as a whole (the incorporative relationship), a fact which is symbolized by attributing a death within the community to the medicine.

In short, medicines may very well be used to enhance one's own position, but eventually this is seen as a blow to one of the possessor's incorporative relationships. This is part of the ethic of medicines, although we shall see later that in actual cases most medicines are believed to have been procured not simply to improve one's self in an absolute fashion but to enhance one's self in comparison with someone else or to weaken another's vital force—in short, in situations where a dispute already underlies the acquisition of the medicine.

The use of medicines in this manner, for the purpose of spoiling a social relationship or another individual's vital state of being, is called *ogulugulu*. The two most frequently discussed practices which fall under the rubric *ogulugulu* are *akulɛ* ('poisoning') and *atɛdyɛ* ('trapping'). *Akulɛ* is to swallow a lethal medicine placed in food or beer. (Whether all such medicines are poisonous by empirical standards is questionable but in any case irrelevant to the Safwa classification.) *Atɛdyɛ*, which is the same word used to refer to trapping wild animals, involves spreading a medicine, specifically concocted to kill a particular person, across a path which the intended victim uses. To prepare a trapping medicine, the hair, nail parings, faeces, or earth from a footprint of the victim must be used.

While both 'poisoning' and 'trapping' are directed against people, a third malicious medicine, *ihobɛ*, is designed primarily to kill livestock. Only after decimating a family's herds is it then believed to attack the herd-owners with a gradually debilitating condition in which the victims are said to eat but never feel full. *Ihobɛ* medicine is inserted in the bone or horn of a cow or bull, and the whole is buried in the house or cattle byre of the victim.

Ogulugulu is said to be used by those who do not have *itonga* to attack others, although in practice the two powers are employed against entirely different categories of victims. Thus a man generally conceded to possess *itonga* may nevertheless be accused of causing a particular instance of death or disease by means of medicines rather than his mystical power.

Ogulugulu, however, is a double-edged sword. On the one hand, it is considered to be quite a dangerous mode of attack for the user. Because its success depends upon the strength of both the life forces and other medicines involved in the situation, it may conceivably rebound upon its owner at any time. On the other hand, because of the many forces involved, it is relatively easy for a person accused of *ogulugulu* to disclaim responsibility for its results. In cases of *ogulugulu* the responsibility tends to become diffused among several people rather than focused on one (as is the case of attacks by people with bad *itonga*).

The Relationship between itonga *and Medicines*

Although the effects of malicious medicines are always detected by a diviner and thus a person with *itonga*, the use of medicines itself is not considered to be *itonga*. As one informant put it, 'Medicines are not like *itonga*. We can see medicines.' Medicines thus constitute a 'visible' cause of disease and death in Safwa terms. No matter how mystical or improbable *ogulugulu* may seem to the Western observer as a cause of disease or death, it is a natural and comprehensible one to the Safwa.

Although medicines and *itonga* are conceived as being different by the Safwa, there is nevertheless a relationship between them. Just as medicines enhance the life state of individuals who are ill or spouseless, they may also enhance one's power of *itonga*. Thus an informant described one compound head in the community as having much *itonga* (*itonga ligɔsi*) because he had many medicines made from the faeces, urine, and footprints of others. When I asked him if it was the medicines which gave the man *itonga*, he replied no, that the man had been born with *itonga* and that the medicines had only strengthened it. This interpretation was later confirmed by other informants.

Empongo *Diagnosed by Autopsy*

Ofubanye
This condition (also called *olupalala* from *empalala*, a kind of spear) is diagnosed by the presence of blood in the bile. This blood is drawn out of the gall bladder during autopsy. The condition is believed to occur when a man kills a member of another lineage from a different community and a member of the murderer's lineage eats or drinks together with a person of the victim's lineage before the proper rituals have been performed to settle the offence.

Proper settlement of a murder requires (1) that the murderer's lineage supply one of their women as wife for a member of the victim's lineage[4] and (2) that all members of both lineages perform a ceremony of reconciliation (*embungo eyɛlupalala*). For this ceremony members of the two lineages congregate at a place where two paths meet. They are accompanied by a medicine man who, from having gone through the same ceremony as one of the principals, knows the proper ritual and medicine to prevent further recurrences of the sickness. The ritual entails a member of each lineage grasping one side of a dog and then a sheep, while another member of either lineage cuts the animal in half longitudinally. Pieces from each half of the two animals are then mixed together with medicine and cooked. All members of both lineages are expected to eat the resulting preparation. Other people who are not directly involved in the feud may also witness the ceremony and partake of the food. After eating, everyone returns home except the medicine man, the girl to be given in marriage, and her father's sister. They proceed to the compound of the father or older full brother of the person who was murdered and again drink medicine to enable the girl to prepare fire in the house where she will cook. The girl is then left with her new family.[5]

Olupɛmbɛ
Olupɛmbɛ is actually a medicine, which is prepared by a medicine man at the behest of a creditor. It is a specific for causing death within

[4] If no suitable female is available or the principals themselves refuse to be married, the murderer's lineage may supply bridewealth for a male of the victim's lineage to procure a bride elsewhere. While this procedure is functionally equivalent to the other in settling the feud, it is felt to be somewhat less satisfactory, since the bond between the two lineages is not welded by the birth of children.

[5] I did not observe the reconciliation ceremony. The above description derives from reports by two men who had participated in them some time ago.

the lineage of a particular debtor and may strike down any member at random, though the strength of a potential victim's *inzyongoni* in relation to the strength of the medicine is thought to influence who the particular victim will be. The medicine is said to be detected post mortem by drawing bile out of the gall bladder and finding fine grains of powdered medicine (*empenga*) and castor beans mixed in it. The condition may also be diagnosed in a living victim by a diviner.

The only way to stop *olupɛmbɛ* from annihilating the debtor lineage is for the creditor and members of the delinquent lineage to go before the medicine man who prepared the concoction. There they must reach a mutually agreeable settlement of the debt, at which time the medicine man will then deactivate his nostrum.

Olupɛmbɛ is used only for debts of a certain kind, those termed *amaxɔlɛ* (singular *ixɔlɛ*). *Amaxɔlɛ* involve money and/or livestock only and involve only members of different lineages. Consequently *olupɛmbɛ* medicine is employed exclusively between members of different lineages in a transactional relationship.

Endasa

One knows that a person has died from *endasa* when post-mortem examination reveals cuts on the liver and blood in the abdominal cavity. (The word *endasa* comes from the verb 'to spear', *alasɛ*.) Only people who possess *itonga* can die from this cause, and the condition shows that the victim had engaged in an unsuccessful battle with another person possessing this power.

Other Causes of Empongo

Amaya

Although *amaya* is never the initial cause of a person's *inzyongoni* becoming weakened, it exacerbates a pre-existing condition of debilitation. It is thus like complications in Western medical parlance. *Amaya* sets in when a sick person is visited by a patrilineal kinsman with whom either he or another resident of his compound has quarrelled and severed relations. The affliction is usually diagnosed by other members of the compound, although occasionally a diviner is consulted to confirm the lay diagnosis. The only way to eliminate this complication is for the residents of the compound to pray to the ancestors together with the offending kinsman, which implies of course a resolution of the original dispute.

ITONGA AND WITCHCRAFT, MEDICINES AND SORCERY: A COMPARATIVE VIEW OF SAFWA BELIEFS

Given this summary of Safwa concepts about the causes of disease and death, one is faced with the problem of fitting them into the larger context of African belief. We wish to concentrate here on the Safwa notions of *itonga* and medicine.

Itonga *and African Witchcraft*

In many respects the *abitonga* clearly resemble the witches of other African societies. Their powers are innate and can harm people, and witchcraft is used to account for misfortunes. Since the Safwa concept of *itonga* thus fulfills these minimal requirements of the definition of witchcraft proposed by Middleton and Winter and recapitulated above in the Introduction, we shall henceforth consider it as a member of this analytic class. We shall nevertheless continue to use the term *itonga* in the Safwa context and only employ 'witchcraft' in discussion of comparative, analytic problems.

In one important respect, however, *itonga* and witchcraft seem quite different. For, apart from the one example of the Nyakyusa (noted in footnote 1 above), anthropologists have tended to portray African witches as by definition antisocial—an attribute which, as we have seen, is not characteristic of the *abitonga*. Our purpose in this section is to show that, appearances to the contrary, the Safwa are not alone with their neighbours the Nyakyusa in believing that the mystical power of 'witches' is morally neutral, and that perhaps the ethnocentric preconceptions of ethnographers are responsible for the dim light in which African 'witches' have traditionally been painted.

In speaking of witchcraft in Africa, one begins almost by necessity with Azande belief. On the matter of the moral implications of Zande witchcraft, Evans-Pritchard is quite clear: 'The Zande phrase "It is witchcraft" may often be translated simply as "It is bad".... A man must first hate his enemy and will then bewitch him' (1937:107). Elsewhere Evans-Pritchard says,

> To Azande themselves the difference between a sorcerer and a witch is that the former uses the techniques of magic and derives his power from medicines, while the latter acts without rites and spells and uses hereditary psycho-psychical powers to attain his ends. *Both alike are enemies of men*, and Azande class them together. (1937:387; emphasis mine.)

70 *Witchcraft, Sorcery, and Social Categories Among the Safwa*

Thus according to the ethnographer, it would seem that Zande witches are by definition anti-social.

If we examine Zande belief more closely, however, this interpretation becomes doubtful. The Zande term *mangu* is translated by Evans-Pritchard (1937:9) as (1) 'witchcraft-substance', a physical entity present inherently in the bodies of certain people; (2) 'witchcraft', the injurious psychic emanation from witchcraft-substance; and (3) 'witchcraft-phlegm', a substance in the bodies of witch-doctors which is produced by medicines and which the witch-doctors claim to be entirely different from witchcraft-substance. That the witch-doctors' claim is not recognized by ordinary Azande is quite clear from Evans-Pritchard's later statement:

> The layman is not entirely convinced by this subtle distinction [between witchcraft-substance and witchcraft-phlegm] and prefers to state plainly that it is ordinary *mangu* in their own bellies which enables successful practitioners to see it in the bellies of others. It is said that there are two kinds of witch-doctors, those who possess magic but are not talented, and the talented ones who possess both medicines and witchcraft.[6] I have many times heard people openly say that successful witch-doctors are witches. A man would not deliberately offend a practitioner by casting this opinion in his teeth, but I have heard Azande, especially princes, chaffing witch-doctors about their witchcraft. It is one of the traditional ideas associated with the corporation [of witch-doctors]. Every one knows it. (1937:187.)

Clearly most Azande believe that both witches and witch-doctors possess the identical power (*mangu*). Moreover, they believe that this power is what enables witch-doctors to divine the activities of witches.

> The skill of a witch-doctor depends on the quality of the medicines he has eaten *and* on his possession of *mangu*. If he is not himself a 'witch' nor has eaten powerful enough medicines he will be a witch-doctor only in name. (1937:219; emphasis mine.)

Witness also the following paraphrase by Evans-Pritchard (1937: 187) of an informant's statement:

> He was convinced that some witch-doctors were genuine and could tell you their names. These genuine practitioners might make mistakes, but they possessed excellent medicines which gave them real prophetic powers, and, above all, they possessed *mangu* (witchcraft-substance). He believed

---

[6] Cf. the Safwa distinction between 'medicine men' and 'diviners'.

that only those practitioners who are themselves witches can observe and control witchcraft. Only through Beelzebub can you cast out devils. ...

Zande doctrine holds that one witch can see another witch and observe what he is doing in the world of witchcraft. ... Hence, a witch-doctor who is also a witch may be relied upon to give correct information about his companions.

In short, on closer scrutiny Azande belief does not appear to differ significantly from that of the Safwa. *Mangu*, like *itonga*, seems to be a neutral power which can be used to effect both moral and immoral ends. On the one hand it may be used to detect and control malevolent people with mystical power; on the other hand it may be used antisocially to sicken or kill one's enemies.

Only if we dismiss the generally accepted Zande view and espouse the witch-doctors' perspective, does there appear to be a difference between Zande and Safwa ideology. For if the *mangu* of witch-doctors is truly 'another thing' from the *mangu* of witches, as the doctors claim (p. 225), then this power may indeed have only immoral effects, as Evans-Pritchard avers. Yet if we accept this viewpoint, we are confronted by serious problems in connection with his entire analysis. On the one hand Evans-Pritchard claims that *mangu* is an inherited substance and uses this attribute to differentiate *mangu* from another key Zande concept *ngua*, which is not inherited and achieves its effects through medicines. However, the witch-doctors claim that their *mangu* is not inherited but comes from medicines, an assertion which clearly controverts the basic distinction drawn between *mangu* and *ngua*. Surely something is amiss here. Either Evans-Pritchard's understanding of the basic distinction between *mangu* and *ngua* is erroneous, or the witch-doctors' claim that their *mangu* comes from medicines is specious and demands further investigation. It would seem that Evans-Pritchard accepted the witch-doctors' claim without probing its implications, because he already had a predilection for viewing *mangu* as entirely anti-social and could not accept the generally reported fact that the same *mangu* that 'bewitches' also detects. In short the Zande data would suggest that *mangu* is a morally neutral power, although this fact is somewhat obscured by the ethnographer's interpretation.

Let us turn now from this classic of African witchcraft and sorcery to the work which provides the point of departure for this book—Middleton and Winter's *Witchcraft and Sorcery in East Africa*. In this work, too, the authors seem to prejudge witches adversely. At

72 *Witchcraft, Sorcery, and Social Categories Among the Safwa*

one point the editors (p. 8) refer to witches as 'personifications of evil, as innately wicked people who work harm against others', and many of the individual contributors to the volume similarly portray witches as anti-social and immoral—even in some cases when their own data suggest another interpretation. Let us examine two of these cases.

Beidelman, reporting on the Kaguru of Tanzania, glosses the term *uhai* as 'supernatural powers' (Beidelman 1963:61) and says, 'The word for witch usually used by Kaguru is *muhai*' (1963:63).[7] According to Beidelman (p. 62), Kaguru 'believe that knowledge of any *uhai* can be used for either social or anti-social ends', but that the use of *uhai* 'may provide the training and encourage the tastes which can lead to night-dancing'. Night-dancing is an attribute of certain possessors of *uhai*, the *wakindi*, who 'enjoy the bad things they do'.

So far the facts sound very much like the situation among the Safwa. The Kaguru believe: (1) in the existence of a group of people who possess supernatural powers which they may use for either social or anti-social ends (the counterpart of the Safwa *abitonga*), and (2) that within this group there are some individuals, the night-dancing witches, who use their powers exclusively for immoral purposes (the direct parallel to people with bad *itonga* among the Safwa). The only difference between Safwa and Kaguru belief seems to be that the Kaguru have a special term for people with mystical powers who use them anti-socially, while the Safwa do not.

Beidelman, however, stresses the anti-social aspects of the behaviour of *wahai* (plural of *muhai*) in his exposition and often fails to make clear whether he is talking about all *wahai* or just the night-dancing *wakindi*. Thus his statement (p. 67) that 'a witch's behaviour is inverted physically, socially, and morally' directly contradicts his previous assertion that people with *uhai*, i.e. 'witches', can use their powers for either social or anti-social ends. It would seem that Beidelman has a predisposition to stress the anti-social activities of the *wahai* and thus distorts the Kaguru situation.

As described by Middleton, the Lugbara of Uganda do not seem to believe in an individual power which causes people harm but in a 'sentiment' which can cause people to bring illness or death to others. Thus,

[7] This latter statement seems a very strange one for an ethnographer to make, since it clearly implies the priority of the ethnographer's own native or theoretical category over that of his informants.

Safwa Aetiological Categories

Lugbara believe that there are several categories of persons who can harm other people in mystical ways not understood by ordinary men. They do so for various evil motives of their own. The means of causing sickness, disaster and even death vary, but the general motive is considered to be envy or jealousy, the sentiment which Lugbara call *ole* (Middleton 1963:261).

Ole is thus defined here as an 'evil motive' and translated by the pejorative terms 'envy' and 'jealousy'. Later, however, we discover that lineage heads call upon the help of the ancestors to discipline junior members because of this same sentiment.

The term used for the activity of a night-witch is *ole rozu*, the same term that is used for the invocation of the dead. I use the two English expressions—to bewitch and to invoke—whereas Lugbara use only one. . . . *Ole* is the sentiment of indignation felt by a senior man when a junior commits a sinful offence. . . . Ghost invocation is good, witchcraft is evil (1963:268).

Obviously again we have a situation where a single entity, this time conceived as a sentiment rather than a power, can be used for either philanthropic or misanthropic ends. It seems to be only the ethnographer's preconceptions which force him to bisect this entity. Although he does call the reader's attention to the unity of the concept in Lugbara, we might have profited from a detailed consideration of the implications of the relationship between the two aspects of the concept. This relationship becomes the more intriguing when we read,

. . . there are certain people who wish it to be believed that they can practise witchcraft. I have never heard it said that a man would wish to be known as a sorcerer, but many have said that a man wishes to be important and to be feared by others. Since the power of witchcraft is the converse of the power of kinship authority and the ability to influence other men, some men who wish to be influential—and this applies particularly to those whose genealogical position handicaps them in acquiring high status—would wish to be thought to have this power, *which they may use for good or for evil* (Middleton 1963:273; italics mine).

Surely this bisection of *ole* into witchcraft and ghost invocation and the assignment of each half to separate compartments is a function of the ethnographer's thinking and not the Lugbaras'.

Unlike the two authors cited above, other contributors to the Middleton and Winter volume explicitly describe a situation much

74 *Witchcraft, Sorcery, and Social Categories Among the Safwa*

like the Safwa, with mystical power being used for both moral and immoral purposes. Thus among the Nandi,

> The *ponindet* ['witch'; plural, *ponik*] bewitches people mainly for his or her own purposes, that is, revenge, greed, or sheer malevolence. Sometimes he does so on behalf of others, for people do resort to *ponik* to obtain satisfaction from those who have injured them. . . .
> The *orkoiyot* of Nandi, the head of the laibon section of the Talai clan and the man recognized by the tribe as their chief ritual expert, also makes use of *ponisiet* ['witchcraft'] on occasion as his prerogative to punish offenders in this way. . . . The chief *orkoiyot* is a *jorindet* ['witchfinder'] as well, that is, he combines in himself the two functions of witchcraft and anti-witchcraft (Huntingford 1963:178).

Among the Mbugwe, as described by Gray, two powers are recognized: *osave* and *wanga*. People with *wanga* not only perform anti-social magical acts but use their power to divine and to prepare beneficial or protective magic as well. *Osave*, on the other hand, 'is always evil in character' (1963:143). Moreover, there is a 'cynical belief that all *vaanga* [people with *wanga*] are also *vasave* [people with *osave*]. The reverse of this is not true, however—all *vasave* are not necessarily *vaanga*' (1963:144). These notions parallel very closely ideas which the Safwa hold about people with good and people with bad *itonga*. Thus the former are always subject to the suspicion that they also practise anti-social acts, while the latter are never mistaken for defenders.

Lest the reader think that this notion of a neutral mystical power, which can be used for both moral and immoral ends, is confined in Africa only to the eastern sector, let us examine an example from West Africa—the Tiv of central Nigeria. The Tiv believe in the existence of a power, *tsav*, which grows on the hearts of certain individuals. This power has a dual aspect: on the one hand, it enables a man to control others and keep the peace; on the other, it may be nourished by cannibalism and thus causes death. (Bohannan 1957, 1958; Price-Williams 1962.) As the ethnographer says by way of summary:

> *Tsav* is itself morally neutral, to be used either for good or for evil. It becomes good if the person is good and nurtures it through good deeds—what we in the West would call 'public service'. It becomes bad if the person is disliked, distrusted, and self-seeking: Tiv say that such a man has nurtured his *tsav* by a diet of human flesh. (Bohannan 1965:540.)

Safwa Aetiological Categories

Although the details are different, the substance of the belief is obviously similar to that of the Safwa. Public leaders (for the Safwa, read 'important heads of compounds') may use their power to uphold or defend the community or to destroy life for their own ends.

This brief and by no means exhaustive survey clearly shows that the Safwa and Nyakyusa are not alone among African peoples in having a concept of a mystical power which can be used for both socially beneficial and maleficent ends. It also apprises one of the dangers of terming this power 'witchcraft' with the load of negative connotations which this term bears in Western tradition. We suggest that viewing a person with mystical power who harms others as necessarily evil is a predilection born of our own Western witchcraft traditions where the category 'witch' necessarily has the attribute 'anti-social' attached to it. Among the Safwa, however, this attribute does not cling to the category *omwitonga*. For the Safwa the question of whether or not a given individual is an *omwitonga* is quite separate from the question of whether he acts anti-socially (*-nandy-*, *-tul-*) or not.

Safwa Medicines and African Magic

Although ethnographers of African peoples have been negligent in describing the use of personal mystical powers for moral purposes, they have long noted the use of medicinal substances for both beneficial and maleficent ends. Again dating from Evans-Pritchard's seminal work, the terminology for the various uses of medicine has become standardized in African ethnographic literature. 'Magic' has been adopted to refer to the use of medicines in general, regardless of purpose; while the term 'sorcery' has been reserved for their use for immoral ends. No standard term has been adopted specifically for the use of medicines to effect moral aims, and Evans-Pritchard himself simply speaks of 'good magic' or 'good medicines'.

Yet neither 'magic' nor 'sorcery' quite conveys the spirit of Safwa belief, since both terms smack of supernaturalism. For the Safwa, medicines do not act in a mysterious way—their action is visible and comprehensible. In fact this is one of the main distinctions between medicines and *itonga*, as we have noted above. The point here is not whether the Safwa 'really' know how medicines work but that they *think* they know. This fact should certainly influence our ethnographic approach to the subject.

This criticism may sound like a mere quibble over labels; and it would be, if labels did not have a profound effect on our thinking about these matters. For by lumping both witchcraft and magic together through the common feature of supernaturalism, ethnocentrically defined, we tend to look for a common logic behind both activities, when this may not be the case. It is manifestly not so for the Safwa, as we shall show.

To avoid the supernatural implications of the traditional terminology, when operating strictly within the Safwa context, we shall speak of the use of medicines and qualify this, as necessary, to indicate either malicious or philanthropic intent. When we move to the analytic level in Chapter VI, however, we shall perforce adopt the traditional terminology. The reader should nevertheless bear the distinctive quality of Safwa medicines in mind.

CHAPTER IV

AETIOLOGICAL CATEGORIES AND THE DIAGNOSIS OF EMPONGO

In the previous chapter we considered the repertoire of possible causes of *empongo*. We shall now examine how the lexical alternatives discussed previously are put to use in concrete instances of *empongo*. We shall be attempting here to answer the following question: given an instance of *empongo*, what aspects of the extra-linguistic environment determine which linguistic alternative will be assigned to the instance as a cause. Although this is essentially a question in semantics, our analysis will frequently raise matters of pragmatic significance. A more complete discussion of the pragmatics of assigning causes to cases of *empongo* must await the following chapter, however.

NATURE OF THE DATA

The data for this analysis consist primarily of cases of disease or death which occurred during the ethnographer's stay in Mwanabantu tribe. Cases which antedated this visit were usually collected only if they were conceived as historically related to contemporary events by the actors involved. This procedure was followed to ensure that the data were collected in the natural context which made them meaningful to the participants. Several initial attempts to elicit case material from the past under abnormal conditions—i.e. by asking questions in a conversational setting without provocation that was locally meaningful—produced bare facts about accusations or divinations but nothing about the tensions or disputes underlying them.

In the process of collecting these data, the writer attempted to get at least two informants to discuss each case and noted differences in interpretation when these occurred. Although a number of ethnographers of African peoples have noted that a single instance of disease or death may evoke from different members of the community a number of different interpretations as to its cause (Douglas 1963: 129–30; Evans-Pritchard 1937:129), none to our knowledge has examined these variant interpretations systematically. This fact is particularly startling because the basic assumption among most writers on the subject of witchcraft is that this presumed cause of death and illness reflects social tensions. Since tensions are usually diffuse, it would seem highly important to collect the variant interpretations of individual instances of disease or death which presumably stimulate expression of these pre-existing tensions. As we shall see in the following analysis of case histories, the data on variant interpretations contribute much to our understanding of the uses to which diagnoses about the causation of disease or death are put.

The matter of collecting variant interpretations raises another point which has often been neglected by many writers on witchcraft and sorcery—namely, the immediate context of accusations. In the United States, for example, it is one thing for a private citizen to say to an acquaintance that the President is incompetent. It is another thing for him to convey this opinion to his Congressman. And it is quite another thing for the Congressman to express this same opinion on the floor of the House. In short, from our own sociological folk-knowledge we know that the immediate social context of an accusation is a very important datum. Yet in anthropological considerations of witchcraft and sorcery, this rather elementary fact has frequently been ignored.

For example, Marwick's elaborate statistical analyses (1952, 1963, 1965) distinguish between cases in which the sorcerer's accuser is known and those in which the 'sorcerer [is] designated by diffuse gossip' (Marwick 1965:106). Yet in cases of the first category we are never informed of how and where an accusation has been made. Most of the older literature on witchcraft and sorcery (e.g. Krige 1947; Wilson 1951, 1963; Nadel 1952) also suffers from this deficiency, although the best recent examples of the so-called 'extended case study' method (e.g. Turner 1957; Middleton 1960) contain these relevant details, the full importance of which we shall observe in the following analysis of Safwa cases.

It is important to note that the time in which this field work was done was a period of political change in Safwaland. When I arrived in the field in October 1962, Tanganyika had been independent only ten months. The Government was still making do with the old British administrative system of Chiefs[1] and Jumbes. Then in

[1] Throughout this book the capitalized term 'Chief' refers to the British-created office, and the term with a lower-case letter refers to the traditional office of head of the tribal lineage.

Aetiological Categories and the Diagnosis of Empongo 79

December 1962, the country declared itself a republic and abolished the old system. A new administrative hierarchy was established, and a conscious policy was followed to employ people from foreign tribes to administer each local area. In addition, judicial and executive roles were split for the first time, with the Chief's judicial functions assumed by local Magistrates and his executive duties by Local Executive Officers. In speeches at Republic Day celebrations and later at local rallies, Government representatives emphasized that the day of the Chief and the local headman were over.

In short, the period of field work was one of considerable flux in the allocation of responsibility for leadership. This situation undoubtedly influenced the incidence and kinds of disputes which were handled through divinatory procedures, although the absence of any statistics on cases submitted for divination at other periods makes this impossible to verify.

CASE STUDIES IN THE CAUSATION OF *EMPONGO*

In the following case material we shall focus on actual instances of *empongo* as the most common natural stimuli for remarks about *itonga*, medicines, and its other causes. Our present interest is to understand the defining features of a situation which cause Safwa to assign one of the various causes, which we described in the previous chapter, to an instance of disease.

We must first clarify the class of terms upon which we shall focus this analysis. In the previous chapter we presented a complete contrast set (Conklin 1964; Sturtevant 1964:108–10), the universe of terms used to diagnose *empongo* in divinatory and post-mortem settings. We note, however, that '*amaya*' and *empongo* attributed to the ancestors' (*empongo ezyangolobɛ*) are somewhat special as members of the contrast set because they are secondary or derivative causes of *empongo*. Thus, only an individual who is already ill may become subject to the complications of *amaya*. And, although ancestors may cause illness directly, they also exert their influence secondarily by exacerbating a pre-existent condition through failing to inform their descendants of the cause. In a sense, too, the ancestors may be viewed as the ultimate cause of all *empongo*, because a descendant only suffers affliction when his ancestors relinquish their protection and watchfulness, as we already observed.

The category *empongo ezyangolobɛ* is thus such a broad term that it may be appended to any other kind of diagnosis, just as *amaya* may also be so appended. For clarity, therefore, we shall concentrate the present analysis on the primary diagnostic categories: *itonga*, with its various manifestations, and medicine. We shall discuss the use of the two secondary categories in the following chapter, however.

The format for presentation of these cases is to recount each one in some detail first, with as little comment or interpretation as possible, and then to follow each account with a commentary on its implications for our problem. The division of most cases into incidents is designed to facilitate exposition; the divisions do not necessarily represent Safwa notions about the fragmentation of the time stream. Those cases or incidents which occurred during our stay in the field are indicated by an asterisk.

Cases Involving Medicine and -ly- as Causes of empongo

Case I: Death of a Watchman*

Mwalyego was a man of about 55 whose wife had died some years ago and whose children were grown. He had never remarried and lived beside his adult, married son in a compound adjacent to those of his widowed mother and his brothers Nalama and Mlavizi. These people formed a corporate economic unit by working their father's *eshiipa* unsubdivided. The yield from the *eshiipa* was kept in granaries located halfway between the mother's and Nalama's (the eldest son's) houses.

Mwalyego held a job as night watchman in a shop in Itimba and daily walked the ten miles each way to work. One morning he returned with his stomach painfully distended and died that night. The funeral was attended by the newly appointed Local Executive Officer, a Nyakyusa, who happened to be in the community that day because there was to have been a meeting to discuss a self-help scheme. Because of his presence, no autopsy was performed, although Mwalyego's mother demanded one and had to be forcibly restrained from throwing herself into her son's grave to prevent his interment without one.

That evening Mwangote, who also held a job in Itimba, told me that 'people' in town were saying that Mwalyego had been killed by a medicine administered by Sayɔta, another night watchman also from Ipepete. It was said that Sayɔta wanted not only Mwalyego's job but also intended to take over the jobs of all the night watchmen on the particular block where Mwalyego had worked (a complete impossibility). I later hear this same story, however, from another person who worked in town.

On the other hand, in a 'saloon' about six miles from Ipepete, where Mwalyego used to stop on his way home from work, another story was circulating: Mwalyego had been stealing from someone in that community, and the person who was being robbed had secured a medicine against theft which had killed the culprit. The saloon was located in a Nyakyusa settlement on the edge of Itimba.

About a week after Mwalyego's funeral his younger brother Mlavizi took over his job as night watchman. Rumours began circulating among those who worked in town that Mlavizi had 'poisoned' (*-kul-*) his brother in order to get his job. In the village, however, he was believed to have consumed (*-ly-*) his brother for the same purpose. Since Mlavizi drank a lot and was often late for work, he soon lost the position, and these rumours died down.

Although I tried to gather further information about this case for several months I heard nothing until two weeks short of a year after Mwalyego's burial. During that year Mwalyego's sons had consulted diviners twice, and Nalama had also gone to two diviners with Mlavizi. Three times diviners said that Mlavizi was innocent, but the fourth diviner said that he had consumed (*-ly-*) his brother. Since he had announced this verdict while Mlavizi had gone to fetch a hot coal to light a cigarette, Mlavizi protested that the divination and the diviner were not reputable. Because of the content of the divination, however, Nalama demanded that the practitioner be paid by Mlavizi, who refused. It was this issue which led to the case being brought to the elders. The elders upheld Mlavizi and laughed at the circumstances of the divination. They inquired, however, into the reasons why so many divinations had been sought. Nalama then accused Mlavizi of having killed a bull of his by unspecified (but presumably supernatural) means, but Mlavizi denied having ever heard of this charge until after the divination. This was a particularly damaging statement for Nalama's case, because it showed that he had not discussed his suspicions openly with his brother before carrying the matter to the elders, a procedure which violated lineage ethics.

The elders reprimanded Nalama, calling him a mischief-maker (*ompugusi*), and told the two brothers to bring them 100 shillings in order to consult Chikanga, a reputed disciple of the famous

Malawian diviner of the same name and the practitioner of highest stature in the Itimba area. So far as I know, this diviner was never consulted. This in fact was the intent of the elders, one of whom explained to me afterwards that they knew that the brothers could not raise that sum of money and considered Nalama a harmless trouble-maker anyway. The decision had merely been intended to mollify him but to leave the way open for further discussion should relations between the brothers worsen.

Commentary on Case I. Although the data in this case consist mostly of rumours, these rumours are very instructive. A summary of the various interpretations of Mwalyego's death is compiled in Table III.

TABLE III

SUMMARY OF INTERPRETATIONS OF MWALYEGO'S DEATH

Interpreters	Person Considered Responsible	Method
(1) 2 men who worked in Itimba	Sayɔta, a resident of Ipepete who also worked in Itimba	medicine
(2) Saloon gossip (mixed Safwa and Nyakyusa patrons)	Nyakyusa from whom Mwalyego had been stealing	medicine against thieves
(3) Gossip among town workers	Mlavizi (Mwalyego's younger brother)	medicine (-*kul*-)
(4) Ipepete gossip	Mlavizi (Mwalyego's younger brother)	-*ly*-
(5) Diviner consulted by Mwalyego's older brother	Mlavizi (Mwalyego's younger brother)	-*ly*-

First it is clear that the cause assigned to a death does not necessarily correlate with the patient's physical state. Thus Mwalyego's bloated stomach was seen by some as caused by medicines and by others as caused by *itonga* (-*ly*-). The cases we shall discuss below also demonstrate that the same physical symptom may be assigned to diverse causes. Moreover these causes also demonstrate the converse condition—viz. the same cause may be assigned to illnesses characterized by very different physical symptoms. (Compare Cases I and VI, for example.) Discussion of these cases with informants led me

Aetiological Categories and the Diagnosis of Empongo

to conclude that the cause assigned to a case of *empongo* is determined by factors outside the patient, rather than by his physical state.

To begin discovering what factors determine the assignment of a cause, let us refer back to Table III. Obviously there is a correspondence between the interpreter and the cause of death he proposes. Thus interpretations proposed either within or for the Ipepete community saw the victim as consumed by an innate power (-*ly*-). Outsiders conceived the cause in terms of medicines. This held true even when the same person was considered responsible. (See interpretations (3) and (4) above.) Thus a distinctive feature of the total situation which appears to influence the cause assigned to a particular instance of disease or death is the group membership of the assigner vis-à-vis that of the victim.

In order to discover why dwellers of Ipepete might conceive Mwalyego's death in another way from the town-workers, even when both agreed at one point that Mlavizi was the culprit, I discussed the matter with a number of Ipepete residents. It became apparent that they conceived Mwalyego's job as part of his estate and thus an office which had been inherited by Mlavizi after his brother's demise. Thus while Mlavizi held the watchman's job, he was seen as having profited unduly from his brother's estate. Although town workers were not polled on this matter, it is unlikely that they conceived the job in this light. More probably they saw it as a position which was open to all and which Mlavizi happened to get not through inheritance but through the influence of his kin connection with Mwalyego.

It thus seems clear that a person's own social position vis-à-vis a sick or deceased individual influences his particular interpretation of the circumstances causing the *empongo*—in other words, that a person's social position influences his interpretation of the event. This conclusion is of course neither unexpected empirically nor novel theoretically, although—as we noted above—it has not usually been considered carefully in analyses of 'wizardry'.

A second observation which can be made about this case must necessarily be tentative at this point: it seems that the kind of group in which the victim of *empongo* is a member has something to do with the way in which the entire situation is conceived. Thus Mwalyego's case suggests that, when a dispute is conceived as lying within a lineage (here between an older and younger brother), the matter is phrased in terms of -*ly*-; when it is conceived as a competition in which the kin tie is not relevant (i.e., a transactional relationship), then medicine is the mode of expression. Although we have only assumed that the town dwellers saw Mlavizi as a competitor for Mwalyego's job rather than as a younger brother coveting the status of his elder, the town workers' accusation of Sayɔta in terms of medicine tends to substantiate this conclusion as does the diviner's verdict, which was undoubtedly based on the minor conflict between Mlavizi and Nalama.

The next case provides further confirmation of the use of the concepts of -*ly*- and medicines to speak of conflicts within lineage and outside lineage bonds respectively. (For the moment we shall postpone consideration of rumour (2) above, which concerns a member of another ethnic group (Nyakyusa) and theft medicine.)

Case II

Incident 1: The Bridewealth Swindle.*—The daughter of Habaya of Ibala community was betrothed by her father to Mwamatete, the son of Mpɛnza, who was headman's assistant in the neighbouring community of Igamba. Mpɛnza gave a number of cows and goats in part payment of the bridewealth, but the girl later married someone else.

Late in June 1963 I attended a session of hearings before the local Jumbe in which Mpɛnza sought to get his livestock back. Habaya, however, argued that the cows had already been used to acquire a wife for himself and had in turn been given as bridewealth to someone else by his father-in-law. The goats, he asserted, had been killed at funerals. He also claimed to have no cows at the moment and to be completely unable to lay his hands on any. The Jumbe ruled that Habaya would nevertheless have to repay all the livestock plus the increase from the cows. He was given one week before he was to appear again at the Jumbe's with some of the animals, as a token of good faith. He never did so. There was talk of taking him to the Magistrate's court next, but the following incident occurred before this was done.

Incident 2: The Son Dies.*—In the middle of July Mwamatete died suddenly. Three days before his death he had been drinking beer and had sickened on his return home. A post-mortem examination was held at the funeral, and the abdominal cavity was seen to contain 'black blood'—a sign indicative of *endasa*.

Three days later the Jumbe called a meeting at which the headman of Igamba announced that six people in his community had died recently (exact duration unspecified) of *endasa*. (The victims were also not specified, although I was able to learn the names of five, two of whom were close kin of Mpɛnza.) People of Igamba had sent representatives to consult a diviner, but the headman reported never having received word of the results of the divination. The Jumbe said that something must indeed be wrong in Itete (the larger sub-region of which Igamba and Ibala are both a part), and that he would send a delegation along with people from Itete to consult the diviner Chikanga of Itimba. In this delegation were Habaya and his older brother (both of Ibala), Mpɛnza, the son of the Igamba headman, and the local member of the Village Development Committee from Itete (a position in the new system of local administration).

At this point in the case Mpɛnza's sister's son reported to me that 'people' were saying that Habaya was responsible for the boy's death. Both the boy and his father were said to have procured medicines to harm Habaya and his cattle, and Habaya was believed to have secured a medicine in self-defence. It was this medicine which was said to have killed the boy.

The divination by Chikanga took place in late August. When I was told of his finding in early September by the assistant to the headman of Ipepete, the substance of the divination was that Mpɛnza and his half-brother were in a league[2] which had demanded the life of their 'son'. Since they yielded it, the brothers were responsible. Chikanga had sent a note back to the Jumbe requesting that Mpɛnza return with his half-brother in order to drink certain medicines to de-activate their *itonga*.

While this account of the divination was being told me, the assistant's sister-in-law, who was present, interjected the question 'Why would Mpɛnza bear a child and then kill him (-*gody*-, the word used for slaying in our sense of the word and metaphorically for *endasa*)?' There then followed a discussion of the implausibility of Mpɛnza's doing such a thing, even though in other contexts

---

[2] The term most often used for associations of people with *itonga* is *echama*, from the Swahili *chama* 'a club, society, association'. That there is no native Safwa term for this concept seems consistent with the overriding importance of lineage as the ideology of association, but this consistency alone does not explain fully the absence of an indigenous term for this important concept. The use of a borrowed word suggests that the concept itself is also borrowed, although I have no evidence of when or how this may have taken place. I shall hereafter translate *echama* as 'league'.

people would accept without hesitation that a father might consume his own son. (See the general discussion of -*ly*-, pp. 60–2.) My Ipepete informants were finding this a difficult divination to accept. Yet when I asked if Mpɛnza had actually admitted killing the boy, this was treated as an irrelevant question, since after all 'Chikanga has divined that he has done so' (*alaguulɛ ochikanga sheshɔ*). In short, the informants did not question the ability of the diviner in this case, nor did they question Mpɛnza's culpability. For them the implication of the divination was that Mpɛnza had consumed (-*ly*-) his own son. It was this particular interpretation which troubled them about the diviner's message. Several days later I heard similar puzzlement about the divination expressed by a group of Ipepete youths.

It was several months later before I had news of this case again, this time from the Jumbe, who had arranged another divination. He began his account by reiterating the fact that at first Habaya had been suspected of killing Mpɛnza's son, but that Chikanga had said this was not so. The new diviner agreed with Chikanga in this, but differed with the rest of his divination. He claimed that Mpɛnza and his half-brother had obtained a medicine to harm Habaya, and that medicine had turned against their own family, killing young Mwamatete. When I asked if medicines could turn of their own accord, the Jumbe replied that Habaya must have had a stronger medicine which 'sent Mpɛnza's medicine back'. When I pushed further and asked why people had died of *endasa* (a sign of *itonga*) when a medicine was responsible, he replied that he did not know.

Commentary on Case II. To facilitate analysis, Table V presents a summary of the various interpretations of Mwamatete's death.

Both the autopsy operators and the headman of Igamba, who had a hand in making the post-mortem diagnosis to begin with, viewed the death as stemming from *endasa*—a cause of death, be it remembered, which is believed to result from fighting with *itonga*. Chikanga's divination essentially agreed with this interpretation.

Yet the people of Ipepete who were discussing Chikanga's divination found his interpretation difficult to accept. In raising the question of why a father should bear a son and then kill him, people from Ipepete were not showing scepticism about this generally held belief. They were, however, questioning its applicability to this case.

Aetiological Categories and the Diagnosis of Empongo 87

Since they saw the dispute over bridewealth as the reason for the death, the notion of the crossfire of *itonga* seemed irrelevant to them. 'Matters of bridewealth like this are matters of medicine,' one party to the discussion said.

Since the Ipepete people, the Jumbe, and the last diviner were all concerned about the bridewealth dispute and also found medicine the only acceptable explanation of Mwamatete's death, it would appear that there is a relationship between the dispute a Safwa focuses on in

TABLE IV

SUMMARY OF INTERPRETATIONS CONCERNING
THE DEATH OF MPɛNZA'S SON

Interpreter(s)	Person(s) Considered Responsible	Method
(1) Autopsy operators	no one named	*endasa*
(2) Headman of Igamba (at public meeting)	no one named	*endasa*
(3) Mpɛnza's classificatory son	Habaya	medicine (in self-defence)
(4) Chikanga (diviner)	Mpɛnza and his half brother	*itonga*
(5) People of Ipepete—questioned interpretation (3), although they did not give their own interpretation		
(6) Diviner and Jumbe	Mpɛnza, his half-brother	medicine

the external situation and the kind of cause he accepts verbally to account for a death or disease. If this observation is true, we should be able to show that the headman and operators of Igamba had some other dispute in mind when they diagnosed Mwamatete's death as due to *endasa*. The following case, which we stumbled upon almost by accident when it was mentioned obliquely at an ancestor rite, confirms that this was so. Let us review this case first and then interpret it and the previous one in the light of their common content.

Case III

The headmen of Igamba and Ibala both traced their ancestry back to the same grandfather. On the whole these men maintained a close, co-operative relationship, so that outsiders commonly dealt with the two communities as a single unit, Itete, in which the headman of Ibala was senior.

Several years ago, however, two residents of Igamba, without permission, began cultivating some unused fields belonging to residents of Ibala. The matter was brought to the headmen, who ruled that, since seeds had already been planted, the cultivators should be allowed to reap their crops but that the fields would then have to be returned. Although this was done, the following growing season several Igamba residents again cultivated fields claimed by Ibala people.

Soon after, the wife of Mpɛnza died. An autopsy at her funeral disclosed that she had died of *endasa*. This was believed to have been caused by the defenders (*abitonga*) of Ibala who were protecting their fields against encroachment. Although no further incidents of intrusion followed, various other people in both Ibala and Igamba were diagnosed as having died of *endasa*. The defenders of both communities were conceived as waging a 'night war' over the incident of the fields. When Mwamatete died, that made the sixth case of *endasa* in Igamba alone, as the headman announced at the meeting called by the Jumbe.

Despite this war, the headmen of the two communities maintained their close relationship and attempted to settle the dispute. Mwamatete's death and Chikanga's divination provided them with an argument they needed to persuade people to stop bickering over the fields. To them, Chikanga's divination indicated that outsiders (speccifially Mpɛnza's brother, but presumably others as well) had been called in to help the Igamba defenders against Ibala and that the people of Igamba had then been called upon to repay this assistance by killing one of their own residents, Mwamatete. (See 'debts of hospitality', pp. 61–2.)

Confronted with this image of their own self-destruction, the people of Igamba formally agreed to stop planting fields belonging to people of Ibala. To confirm this resolution, the headmen of the two communities arranged an ancestor ceremony for their common forebear.

Commentary on Cases II and III. Although the headman and operators were aware of Mpɛnza's attempt to recover his bridewealth from Habaya, they diagnosed the cause of Mwamatete's death as *endasa*. To some degree this diagnosis was undoubtedly forced on the men by the nature of the symptoms (the suddenness of death and the presence, from all reports, of a considerable amount of blood in the abdominal cavity). Nevertheless the diagnosis was consistent with the pattern of previous Igamba post-mortems and divinations, which had been made with regard to the conflict between the people from Igamba and Ibala over the fields. It is certainly plausible that the 'big men' of Igamba had this dispute in mind, rather than Mpɛnza's dispute with Habaya when they diagnosed *endasa*. It is certainly the dispute which concerned the headman of Igamba in his report to the Jumbe at the public meeting.

Case III therefore supports two observations which we made tentatively in commenting on the previous two examples. First, we observed after Case I that the particular dispute a Safwa focuses on in the external situation influences what kind of cause he will assign verbally to account for a death or disease. Clearly people who focused on the bridewealth dispute preferred medicine as a cause, while those intent on the land dispute preferred *endasa*. Secondly, Cases II and III support the observation, made on the basis of Case I, that a person's own social position influences his interpretation of a given situation involving death or disease. On one hand the elders of Igamba saw the death of Mwamatete as *endasa*, and on the other hand the people of Ipepete saw it as due to medicine.

On the basis of these two observations, we make the additional suggestion that a person's social position is the primary determinant of the particular dispute which he focuses on in the social field. We suggest this by virtue of the following logic. Our previous observations are that both a person's social position and the particular dispute he focuses on influence the cause he assigns to a case of *empongo*. It seems reasonable to suggest that the dispute is an intervening variable and that the causal chain is: a person's social position influences which dispute he focuses on in the social field, and the nature of the dispute in turn influences the type of cause assigned to an instance of *empongo*.

This conclusion is borne out by the clear evidence that the immediate determinant of the cause assigned to a case of *empongo* is the social units involved in the dispute which becomes associated with it. That is, the immediate relationship is between the nature of the dispute and the cause assigned to the *empongo*.

Let us return to Case II and examine the evidence for this conclusion. The Ipepete people who were gathered around the headman's assistant as he related Chikanga's divination to the writer were all roughly in the same social position vis-à-vis the dispute which was being discussed. They were outsiders from another community which was tied to the disputants' communities by the common patrilineal clan membership of their headman. No one present was directly related to the parties involved in the dispute. In accord with our previous observation that a person's social position influences the dispute he will focus on in a particular instance of *empongo*, all these Ipepete informants in fact fixed upon the same dispute: the one between Mpɛnza and Habaya. Since they could not accept Chikanga's interpretation in terms of *itonga* and were more satisfied with an interpretation in terms of medicine (see the quote from one informant above), it seems that there was something in the structure of this dispute which precluded conceptualization in *itonga* terms. Because the dispute was between non-kinsmen from different communities, it had to be a case of medicine in the eyes of the people of Ipepete.

To test this hypothesis at the time, we asked two questions of the headman's assistant and the others gathered around. First, if Mpɛnza and Habaya had been from the same community, would it still seem sensible to suspect that the death had been caused by medicines? And second, what kind of situation might provoke Chikanga's divination? The replies to these questions clearly indicate that the nature of the social units involved in the dispute determine the cause assigned to the case of *empongo* associated with it. Thus, the reply to the first question was that it would not seem right somehow to suspect the use of medicines in this dispute if Mpɛnza and Habaya were from the same community. Furthermore, in answer to the second question, the informants suggested that if Mpɛnza's son had been a 'trouble-maker' in the community or if the defenders of Igamba had been involved in a night war, then Chikanga's divination would make sense to them. Indeed this second interpretation was the one held by people in Igamba and Ibala, as we have seen in Case III.

The Ipepete informants undoubtedly knew of the Igamba-Ibala dispute. Their very suggestion that a night war might have led to Chikanga's interpretation of Mwamatete's death probably indicates their awareness. Certainly the headman's assistant must have known about the land dispute. In view of this, we must consider the question, why did the Ipepete people focus on the bridewealth dispute and publicly, at any rate, ignore the land dispute. We suggest that they did this because to speak of the land dispute, as non-members of the headman's lineage, was presumptuous. This was, after all, a dispute within the headmen's lineage, so to speak, because it involved two communities linked by the patrilineal tie of their headmen. It further-

Aetiological Categories and the Diagnosis of Empongo 91

more concerned a segment of the patrilineage quite remote from their own headman's. We suggest, therefore, that silence was maintained because of the general injunction against speaking about disputes in other patrilineages. We shall discuss these tabus further in the next chapter on pragmatics, where the present discussion more properly belongs.

The significant point for our present discussion, however, is that the Ipepete informants' responses to the questions posed by the ethnographer show that the social units involved in a dispute do indeed influence the way in which it is conceptualized. The following case corroborates this observation.

Case IV
 Incident 1: The Bartered Bride. Mlɔzi was a rather boastful and irrascible man of about 60 who was reputed to possess *itonga*. In about 1956 he secured a medicine for an unknown purpose from a diviner cum medicine man in another Safwa tribe. In return for the medicine, Mlɔzi promised the diviner either his own daughter in marriage or the equivalent bridewealth. The daughter refused the match and eloped with someone else, but Mlɔzi never handed over the promised bridewealth.

When several members of Mlɔzi's lineage died in subsequent years, a relationship was seen between these incidents and the unpaid debt. (See the following incident for details on one such death.) The Chief told me that after three of Mlɔzi's kinsmen had died, he tried to arrange a settlement of this debt, but without success. He explained that he had heard of the divinations through his mother, who was Mlɔzi's sister, and, as Chief, thought he could arrange a settlement.

 Incident 2: A Sister's Demise.* After a long illness Mlɔzi's sister, who was also the mother of the last Safwa Chief, died. During the woman's decline her daughter and a brother's son consulted a diviner in a neighbouring sub-division of Mwanabantu territory. At the funeral a headman from Mwanabantu accused Mlɔzi of being responsible for the woman's death. The diviner had said that because Mlɔzi had not paid his debt, the maker of the original medicine had caused it to strike down members of Mlɔzi's own lineage. He named five other members of the lineage who had also been killed by the medicine. Mlɔzi's own son verified that his father had procured the original medicine, and one of the deceased's sons tried to kill Mlɔzi on the spot but was restrained by the crowd.

Within the next four or five months Mlɔzi was taken to another diviner by Dendɛ (the head of the major lineage of headmen), a son of the deceased, and a member of his own lineage. This diviner confirmed the previous divination and also said that Mlɔzi was not a proper diviner and used his powers to kill people who came to him (i.e. he used his *itonga* for bad rather than good ends). Dendɛ, together with the headman who had originally accused Mlɔzi at the funeral and a member of Mlɔzi's lineage, later took the culprit to his creditor and arranged for him to clear the debt, so that the creditor would stop the medicine from acting. At the time I left the field several months later, this debt had still not been paid.

Several months before leaving the field, however, I had occasion to consult Mlɔzi about something and asked him whether he had drunk a medicine to make him use his powers for good (i.e. to convert his bad *itonga* into good *itonga*). He said he hadn't, but that he had promised never to use them for evil again. He avoided answering questions about the payment of the debt, however.

Commentary on Case IV. It is worth noting that Mlɔzi's sister's death could have been conceived in terms of *itonga* in a fashion completely consistent not only with the general Safwa belief that people with *itonga* attack primarily their own lineage mates but also with the widely accepted opinion in Magombɛ that Mlɔzi himself possessed the requisite powers to do this. Yet instead the death was discussed in terms of medicines.

It is therefore not a simple relationship between the victim and supposed culprit which determines how a case of disease or death will be symbolized. Rather, the significant feature is the social relationship between parties to the particular dispute which becomes symbolized by an instance of death or disease. In other words, in order to explain the occurrence of an illness or death, people in a particular social category focus on one out of any number of disputes which exist simultaneously in the social field. The illness or death comes to stand for the dispute, and the expressed cause of the illness symbolizes the social relationship between the parties to this dispute. Thus in the case above, although the victim and culprit were lineage mates, the death was seen as due to medicines because the dispute which the death symbolized was not within the lineage but between non-kinsmen.

Aetiological Categories and the Diagnosis of Empongo

The following two cases further confirm this conclusion. Although some of the actors in these cases are the same, we have presented the cases separately for analysis because they involve different disputes. The effect of the former case on the latter will be examined in the commentary following the data, however.

Case V: An Ambitious Family

Mpembɛla was a man of *itonga* who had been ostracised from his natal community some time in the latter part of the nineteenth century. He came to Ipepete and was given land to settle there by Old Mwankoshi, then head of a branch of Mwanabantu lineage (q.v., p. 21). Mwankoshi also gave Mpembɛla a wife, a Bungu girl, who had reputedly been found abandoned on a path after an Ngoni march through Safwa country. Mpembɛla had a son Mwashitete who sometime later married the daughter of Mwankoshi's assistant. This couple's eldest son was Ntandala, a man of about 60 at the time of this field work.

Mpembɛla's family prospered in Ipepete, and by the time Mwashitete became head of the lineage, they occupied a large stretch of land, called Mabandɛ, at the eastern edge of Onkoshi's territory. Mwashitete acquired many cattle during his lifetime and became a man of considerable renown in Mwanabantu territory. When he died some time in the late 1940s, Ntandala reputedly killed five head of cattle at the funeral ceremonies and interred his father with a bull—an animal usually reserved for burial only with headmen. Henceforth Ntandala began to run his sector of Ipepete like a separate community. He began by using his *eshiipa* as an *ikwila*—that is, by holding communal beer drinks for all the people of Mabandɛ. He also began inviting other headmen to the ceremonies in honour of his ancestors, an act which could be interpreted as an assertion of membership in the reigning patrilineage. (It is possible that Mwashitete had preceded his son in some of these kinds of independent activities, although no overt strain in relations between Mpembɛla lineage and Onkoshi lineage occurred until Ntandala's time.)

At the time of Ntandala's push for acceptance as a headman in his own right, the headman of Ipepete and the elder of Onkoshi's branch of Mwanabantu lineage was Shabega. A junior branch of the lineage was headed by Lyandile, who was also Chief under the British system of administration. Shabega was a traditionalist, whose power and position depended entirely on his status in the lineage and on his ability, of course, to carry out the roles of that status. Lyandile, on the other hand, was a dynamic personality and aware of the political leverage his Chiefly office gave him in the traditional system.

Some time in the mid-1940s Shabega's grandson, Ndele, the eldest son of his potential successor, became ill with an infected toe. A diviner said that Ntandala had produced the illness by means of a medicine. This was by no means the first divination implicating Ntandala in illnesses among Shabega's branch of the lineage. Soon after this divination Lyandile had Ntandala named Jumbe of Magombɛ, but at the same time he curbed Ntandala's pretensions to membership in Mwanabantu lineage by joining Shabega in the practice of never attending any of Ntandala's ancestor rites. This practice was still maintained at the time of my field work by all members of the Onkoshi minor lineage unless they were also affines of the Jumbe.

Ntandala himself gave me a genealogy in which he made Mpembɛla the son of Old Onkoshi. Many people in Ipepete did not question this interpretation when I asked them about it. To what extent some actually believe it or were simply withholding their beliefs from me, I was unable to determine. Only the last Safwa chief (Lyandile's son and replacement) would tell me openly that the genealogy was false and Ntandala was not a Mwanabantu, although—as I pointed out already—other Onkoshi acted in terms of this fact by not attending Ntandala's ancestor rites.

Case VI

Incident 1: The Asthmatic Jumbe. After Ntandala was appointed Jumbe, his half-brother Mwakingili (who was headman of a subsection of Mabandɛ) was said to have helped him considerably in his work. Ntandala suffered from asthma, and once when he was laid up with an attack, Mwakingili was said to have told people that he would soon take over Ntandala's job. The diviner who was called at that time named Mwakingili as the cause of the disease. He summoned both Mwakingili and his younger brother Kabɛta to drink medicine to stop their half-brother's attacks. Kabɛta appeared, but Mwakingili refused to do so. After that occurrence Ntandala consulted several diviners, including the real Chikanga in Malawi (then Nyasaland). All these men named Mwakingili as the culprit, but Mwakingili consistently refused to appear with Ntandala before a diviner. Furthermore, Kabɛta's compliance with Ntandala's request caused ill feeling to arise between the two full-brothers.

Incident 2: A Mother's Death.* While I was in the field, the mother of Mwakingili and Kabɛta died. She was a very old woman, and informants in Ipepete considered her death to have resulted from old age. Significantly, however, in Mabandɛ an entirely different interpretation of the situation prevailed. About a week after the woman was buried, a rumour began to spread that Mwakingili had consumed (-*ly*-) his mother. So far as I could determine, the source of the rumour was Ntandala, though I never discovered the exact manner in which he initiated it.

Incident 3: An Epidemic among Children.* Between mid-October and mid-December 1963 many children in the Magombɛ area died of either measles or chicken pox. In Ipepete alone I recorded six deaths, and many more children were ill. Dendɛ, Shabega's successor as headman of Ipepete, and senior elder of Onkoshi minor lineage after Lyandile's death, called a meeting of everyone in Magombɛ to be held at the edge of the sacred grove in Ipepete. A large crowd gathered, including all the headmen of the region. Dendɛ conducted the meeting and began by summoning the chiefly ancestors by name and presenting them with the usual list of grievances—the seeds did not germinate, the cows were dry, and women failed to bear children. He then pointed to the fact that many women were walking around with their breasts bared (a sign of mourning for a child), and the headmen present began to discuss the nature of the disease which was sweeping the country. After a brief and inconclusive argument about the exact illness, Dendɛ announced that any woman who knew of tabu sexual activities that were being practised should report them to the headman.

He then asked each headman in turn if all was well in his community. When it came to Mabandɛ, a half-brother of both Ntandala and Mwakingili related a recent flare-up of the old conflict between his half-siblings. Mwakingili was said to have passed a remark that Ntandala was not a Safwa but a Bungu—a statement clearly designed to impugn his brother's right to either a headmanship or a jumbeship in Safwa territory. Ntandala called a meeting of the elders of Mabandɛ to hear this charge, but in spite of witnesses' testimony to the contrary, Mwakingili denied ever making this allegation. He again denied the charge at the plenary meeting, and after further inconclusive wrangling, someone suggested that the day's proceedings continue, since this was not a matter which needed to be discussed in front of everyone. (*Enongwa ezyaxaya yakwɛ.* 'It is a matter for his compound.')

Commentary on Cases V and VI. We shall begin by focusing on the manner in which Ndele's illness was conceptualized in view of the dispute between Shabega and Ntandala over the latter's secession from Ipepete community and self-appointment as a rival headman.

With respect to the social groups involved, this dispute could potentially have been viewed in any one of three ways. First, it could have been seen as a dispute within Ipepete community between the headman and one of the resident compound heads. This view would completely deny Ntandala's secession and was clearly precluded by Ntandala's obvious independence and large following in Mabandɛ. A second interpretation of the dispute could have been that it was one between two headmen of the same patrilineage—that is, two headmen of the same tribe. For Shabega to have interpreted the dispute in this light would have been tantamount to his accepting Ntandala's claim of membership in the Mwanabantu lineage; this interpretation was also unacceptable to him. The remaining interpretation of the dispute was that it was between two rival, unrelated headmen. This was the interpretation favoured by Shabega, and it was symbolized by Ndele's illness in terms of medicine. Thus again, as in Cases II and IV, a dispute between two unrelated parties from different communities was symbolized in terms of medicines.

The dispute between Ntandala and his half-brother Mwakingili, on the other hand, was symbolized by explaining the death of the latter's mother in terms of *-ly-*. This example therefore agrees with Interpretations (4) and (5) of Case I, both of which associated diagnoses of *-ly-* with a dispute between two brothers. It would thus seem that disputes within a lineage are verbalized in terms of *-ly-*. This specific conclusion corroborates the general proposition, advanced previously, that particular causes of disease indicate the social relationships between parties to a dispute.

An additional point should be noted, specifically about Case VI. When *empongo* reach epidemic proportions, a different range of causes is invoked to explain them. During the proceedings outside the *igandyɔ* two such cases were mentioned. First, women were told to

Aetiological Categories and the Diagnosis of Empongo

report cases of *eshitwi* to the headmen. *Eshitwi* is pregnancy occurring as the result of sexual relations consummated during tabu periods—particularly during the time between the death of a child and the mother's first menses. The wholesale violation of tabus on sex was thus conceived as one cause of the epidemic. The other cause was the anger of an ancestor concerning a bull which had been promised him in September and which by December had still not been sacrificed. The ancestor was told, 'Just because we have not done it [sacrificed the bull], it doesn't mean we won't. We are going to do it soon. Don't forget us.' The last statement implies that the epidemic was due to the withdrawal of the ancestors' protection and assistance because of anger over the bull. This implication was later confirmed by a headman when the ethnographer questioned him directly. He further maintained that the violation of sex tabus was above all a cause of the magnitude of the epidemic.

By way of conclusion to this investigation of the causes of *empongo*, we should like to present two more cases in detail. These cases will be seen to form revealing contrasts with some of those previously cited.

Case VII

Incident 1: The Unwilling Father-in-law. Nkɛbeŋa was the headman of Itemba, and his son Mwadala was married to the daughter of Onlaga, a man from another community. Over a period of years several of Mwadala's children died. Each time he consulted a diviner, Onlaga was named as the culprit; and each time he was thus named, Onlaga refused to accompany his daughter and son-in-law to the subsequent divination. (Unfortunately I was unable to learn the manner in which Onlaga was said to have killed his 'grandsons'.) Finally Mwadala decided to divorce his wife and asked Onlaga to return the bridewealth. Since Onlaga never complied, the woman never returned to her father.

Incident 2: A Headman's Death.* In May 1963 Nkɛbeŋa died after a long illness. A diviner had diagnosed the cause as a medicine, prepared from Nkɛbeŋa's faeces by a member of his own lineage. Two days following the funeral at the installation of the new headman, who was Mwadala's classificatory older brother (his father's older brother's son), a discussion occurred concerning another child of Mwadala's who was then sick. The other headmen present told the new headman of Itemba to see to it that Mwadala consulted a diviner. This was never done, however.

Incident 3: The Ancestors Welcome a Kinsman. At the ceremony to mark the entry of Nkɛbeŋa into the land of the ancestor spirits, the chief headman of the Magombɛ-Omwabele area conducted the prayers. In them he accused the new headman of spoiling the compound by not having seen to it that Mwadala consulted a diviner. He accused both Mwadala and Onlaga of being delinquent, but underscored the irresponsibility of the headman in not seeing to it that good feeling had been re-established in the compound. He told all three to put aside any previous divinations and jointly to consult a diviner anew.

Case VIII

About twenty-five years ago there were two full brothers, Ontewa and Mwanzumba, living in Ipepete. Although both brothers reportedly got along well with Shabega, then headman of Ipepete, they quarrelled frequently between themselves. The exact cause of the quarrel was difficult to ascertain, but several informants cited jealousy over Ontewa's closer relationship with Shabega as a reason. (This is probably a formula for expressing the cause of a disagreement which concluded in the manner of this one, the true reason having been forgotten by some informants and withheld by others.)

On several occasions when children of Ontewa died, Mwanzumba was held responsible. Friction between the two brothers was intense when one of Shabega's teenage sons died suddenly. A diviner accused Mwanzumba of having consumed (*-ly-*) him. Ontewa, with the backing of the headman and other elders, placed thorn branches across Mwanzumba's door, a sign that he was no longer welcome in the community. Mwanzumba left with his sons to settle in his mother's natal community.

Commentary on Cases VII and VIII. The importance of these cases for our present investigation lies in their clear demonstration that the victim of a case of *empongo* need not be involved directly in the dispute that becomes associated with his illness or demise. However, he is always a member of a group to which one of the disputants belongs. Thus Nkɛbeŋa himself was not an immediate participant in the dispute between Mwadala and Onlaga, but he was Mwadala's father and thus a close agnatic kinsman. Case VIII demonstrates this point even more clearly in that the headman's son was clearly not one of the prota-

Aetiological Categories and the Diagnosis of Empongo 99

gonists in the dispute between the brothers Ontewa and Mwanzumba; he was, however, a member of the brothers' community.

Conclusions: Cases Involving Medicine and -ly-
Table V summarizes the preceding data, from which emerge our major conclusions as to the distinctive features of the situation with which a Safwa is dealing when he assigns a particular cause to an instance of disease or death. Briefly, an instance of *empongo* comes to symbolize a dispute in the social field, and the particular cause assigned to that instance depends upon the societal units involved in the dispute. The relationship between the victim and culprit does not correlate with the cause of *empongo* diagnosed, but the social relationship between protagonists in a dispute does. The social units in the dispute are therefore the distinctive features to which a Safwa is attuned in making statements about the causes of particular instances of disease or death.

Our specific conclusion from the above cases is that: (1) when the dispute lies within a patrilineage, the cause assigned to the signifying case of *empongo* is *-ly-*; and (2) when the dispute lies between parties who are not patrilineally related and are of different tribal communities, the cause is attributed to medicines. The appendix contains accounts of the remainder of the cases observed, all of which support this conclusion.

Other Causes of empongo

The above conclusion treats only medicines and *-ly-* as causes of *empongo*. What of other causes—namely *-lɔdy-*, *-gun-*, and *endasa*? Unfortunately we could collect only three cases each of *empongo* attributed to *-lɔdy-* and *endasa* and two cases attributed to *-gun-*. Our conclusions concerning the usage of these terms are therefore to be taken with some caution. In drawing conclusions from this small sample of cases, however, we receive additional support from the fact that the cases, although few, are universally consistent with the pattern we have outlined above—viz. that the different terms used to indicate the cause of a case of *empongo* refer to the relationship between the social units involved in a dispute.

-lɔdy-
The three cases in our data which concern a diagnosis of *-lɔdy-* indicate that this cause of *empongo* contrasts with both medicine and

TABLE V

SUMMARY OF CASES HIGHLIGHTING RELEVANT VARIABLES

Formally Diagnosed Cases (Autopsied or Divined)

Interpretations[a]	I					II	III	
	1	2	3	4	5		a	b
Relationship between: Victim / Culprit	coresidents of same community	Safwa / Nya-kyusa	full brothers	full brothers	full brothers	son / father	members of rival communities / defenders	youth / defenders of his community
Parties to underlying dispute	?	Safwa / Nya-kyusa	competitors for job?	full brothers	full brothers	2 men of different communities	two communities of same tribe	two communities of same tribe
Cause of *empongo*	medicine	medicine	medicine	-ly-	-ly-	medicine	*endasa*	*endasa*

TABLE V (*continued*)

Formally Diagnosed Cases (Autopsied or Divined)

Interpretations[a]	IV	V	VI a	VI b	VII a	VII b	VIII a	VIII b
Relationship between: Victim / Culprit	sister / full brother	no relationship	half brothers	mother / son	grand-son / grand-father	agnates	agnates	headman's son / com-moner
Parties to underlying dispute	two men from different communities	unrelated headmen of different communities	half brothers	half brothers	son-in-law / father-in-law	son-in-law / father-in-law	full brothers	full brothers
Cause of *empongo*	medicine	medicine	-ly-	-ly-	?	medicine	-ly-	-ly-

[a] Arabic numbers indicate alternative interpretations of the same case. Lower-case letters indicate different incidents of *empongo* in the same case.

102 *Witchcraft, Sorcery, and Social Categories Among the Safwa*

-ly- by indicating disputes, not between individuals of different lineages and communities or between individuals within a single patrilineage, but between individuals of different lineages of the same community. Let us examine the cases before discussing this cause of *empongo* further. Although the following two cases are related through the person of Mwanaŋwa, who is a key protagonist in both, we shall consider them separately because the dispute and the disputants in each case are quite different. The relationship between the two cases will be discussed in the following chapter, however. (See pp. 123–4.)

Case IX

About fifteen years ago Mwanaŋwa was 'chased' from a village in Omwabele and sought to return to Ipepete, his father's natal village, to establish residence. There was a history of *itonga* in Mwanaŋwa's line, and his own conduct at Omwabele had shown him to possess bad *itonga* himself. But because he was a member of a distant branch of the Mwanabantu chiefly lineage and because of the general practice of accepting *abitonga* as immigrants to help fight alien *abitonga*, Mwanaŋwa was granted land by the present headman (Dendɛ) and settled in Ipepete.

Near his new compound Mwanaŋwa began cultivating a field which was held by Mwasapile, another resident of the community. Although Mwasapile had not cultivated that particular field in over two years and showed no immediate intention of doing so, he disputed Mwanaŋwa's right to work the plot and brought the matter to Dendɛ and the elders. At the moot Mwanaŋwa was not properly apologetic for cultivating the land without permission from the owner. He was, nevertheless, given the right to cultivate the field, although Mwasapile's ultimate title to the land was upheld.

An unspecified time later a kinsman of Mwasapile's (a classificatory father) was serving beer in his compound in Ipepete, and Mwanaŋwa became abusive towards those present. To avoid difficulty, the guests left the house where Mwanaŋwa was drinking. Mwanaŋwa then began talking angrily to the compound head's wife, who had remained behind to serve the beer. Finally the head of the compound was forced to ask Mwanaŋwa to leave. Although the substance of the argument on this occasion was never completely clarified for me, it had something to do with a claim by Mwanaŋwa to permanent title to the disputed farm plot.

Aetiological Categories and the Diagnosis of Empongo 103

After this incident, Mwanaŋwa's reputation for bad *itonga* grew in the community.

In 1962 Mwasapile became ill, and the aforesaid 'father', along with Mwasapile's son and his wife's brother, consulted a diviner. Mwananwa was divined as the cause of the illness. Mwasapile was moved to his mother's father's kinsman in another tribal area, where he died. Later, over a beer basket after a communal working party in Mwanaŋwa's daughter's field, Mwanaŋwa was publicly accused of killing Mwasapile by introducing a foreign substance into his body (-lɔdy-). The accuser was Mwasapile's son. Mwanaŋwa replied to the charge by saying that he would be glad to stand trial before a Government court, if his accusers could find proof of his guilt. He rebuked his accusers for not having summoned the police immediately after the death if they suspected foul play. No further action was taken on this accusation, and during my period of field work Mwanaŋwa was still cultivating the field in question.

Case X

Incident 1: Yacɔbɔ and the Missing Clothes.* Yacɔbɔ, the eldest son of Mwanaŋwa, was betrothed to Wambe, the daughter of Dendɛ (the Ipepete headman). This marriage had been promoted by Wambe's mother and oldest brother, although Dendɛ himself and another brother were said to disapprove of the match.

One day in December 1962 Yacɔbɔ returned to his house and found a pair of trousers and a shirt missing. He suspected a rival for the hand of Wambe of having stolen the clothes and went to Dendɛ to report the theft. He did this because of Dendɛ's status as headman not as his future father-in-law. Dendɛ suggested that Yacɔbɔ consult a diviner. To do so, he travelled to another Safwa tribal area. Since the man he sought there was away in Unyakyusa, however, he instead consulted Kalote, the father-in-law of Wambe's oldest brother. Kalote told him that 'a certain person' living near Mwanaŋwa's compound had stolen the clothing. He described the compound as having about fifteen inhabitants and three houses, the respective locations of which he described in some detail. Yacɔbɔ decided that the description fitted Mwasapile's compound. Kalote suggested that Yacɔbɔ go to another practitioner who could concoct a medicine to make the culprit admit his crime publicly; he also suggested that Yacɔbɔ might consult another diviner nearer home.

Incident 2: Wambe's Fever.* One afternoon in late December Yacɔbɔ came to me to report that Wambe was very sick and asked me if I would take her, her older brother, and him to Kalote, the diviner he had consulted about the clothing theft. Since I was indisposed myself that day, I refused to take them but offered to go to Wambe and see what I could do to help. I found the girl sleeping by the fire. She complained of pains in her head and chest, although observable symptoms, e.g. fever, were slight. Since she did not seem particularly ill, I told her to come with me to my compound where she could stay with her brother's wife. She walked there, a distance of about half a mile, without apparent hardship, and I gave her several aspirin tablets. The next morning she still showed few symptoms. I agreed to go to the diviner but suggested we take her to the hospital first. The hospital refused to admit her as not sick enough.

In Ipepete a rumour began circulating to the effect that certain unspecified people in the community were causing the illness to prevent Wambe from marrying Yacɔbɔ. I also learned from a half-sister of Wambe that the girl herself was now refusing to marry Yacɔbɔ because she 'feared *itonga*'. I could not get the girl to elaborate this statement, although one of my assistants (who was a kinsman of Mwasapile) said that Wambe feared an attack from Mwanaŋwa, her future father-in-law. He would not specify whether the *itonga* would be directed against her by Mwanaŋwa himself or by people who would try to punish Mwanaŋwa through her.

Incident 3: Yacɔbɔ's Eyes.* On the last day of December Yacɔbɔ came to me with an eye infection. I doctored it and learned that he had already treated the condition with the steam from a decoction of certain flowers. After this treatment he had found 'small bones' (*ɔtufupa*) in the water, proof that someone had harmed him by *-lɔdy-*. He suspected his rivals for the hand of Wambe. He told me he had not come to me sooner for treatment because my medicine was effective only after the offending substances had been removed.

Incident 4: A Divination.* Wambe, her parents, older brother and his wife consulted a diviner early in February. He said that a person 'who lives on the other side of a certain stream' and whom Wambe had met once on the path to the lowland fields had a 'bad heart' (evil intent) towards her. Wambe said she did not remember such a meeting and could not identify the person. The diviner then said that Wambe would suffer if she married Yacɔbɔ because his 'father'

Aetiological Categories and the Diagnosis of Empongo   105

(classificatory term: *oyisɛ yɔlumɛ wahɔ*) was working *itonga* against her.

About three weeks later Wambe ran off with another lad from Ipepete. Within three days, return of the bridewealth had been arranged by Dendɛ and Mwanaŋwa and the initial gifts of the new bridewealth given. Several weeks after that, Yacɔbɔ became engaged to another girl.

Commentary on Cases IX and X. The dispute between Mwanaŋwa and Mwasapile over the garden was one between members of different lineages living in the same community, and Mwasapile's death was seen as a case of *-lɔdy-*. Similarly Yacɔbɔ in Incident 3, Case X was harmed by *-lɔdy-* in his contest with another youth from the same community for Wambe's hand. That this contest was in the nature of a dispute rather than simple rivalry is due to the fact that Yacɔbɔ had already given bridewealth for the girl. Although a generalization based on two cases must necessarily be provisional, it would nevertheless seem that, in cases when the dispute which is symbolized by a particular instance of *empongo* concerns parties from different lineages but the same community, the cause of the *empongo* is conceived in terms of the introduction of foreign substances into the body of the victim (*-lɔdy-*). Case XXI (Appendix) affords additional empirical support for this interpretation.

Further corroboration comes from three kinds of evidence. First, this interpretation is consistent with the pattern that we have observed with regard to *-ly-* and medicines—viz. like these terms, it refers to certain social units between which there is a dispute that comes to be symbolized by a particular instance of disease or death. Second, the evidence for this interpretation is internally consistent—i.e. the three cases of *-lɔdy-* all concern precisely the same kinds of social units. And third, the manner in which *-lɔdy-* is conceived is structurally similar to the conception of the community (*empaŋa*), the social unit with which it is equated. In other words, the position of *-lɔdy-* with respect to *-ly-* and medicines is parallel in structure to the position of the community vis-à-vis the lineage and the absence of kinship connection. Thus *-lɔdy-* is like *-ly-*, the cause of *empongo* symbolic of within-lineage strife, in that both are caused by the power of *itonga*. Yet unlike *-ly-*, *-lɔdy-* involves physical substances, much like medicines (the cause of *empongo* symbolic of strife between non-kinsmen). Structurally, then, *-lɔdy-* is intermediate between *-ly-* and medicines, being classed with the former but possessing certain attributes of the latter. In a parallel fashion the community—the social unit with which *-lɔdy-* is symbolically associated—is intermediate between no kinship connection at all and the lineage. Thus the community is conceived within the framework of lineage ideology (as we have already observed in Chapter I), but at the same time involves sub-units which are completely unrelated. In short, the structural position of *-lɔdy-* on the level of the ideology of disease causation exactly parallels the structural position of its *designatum*, the community, on the level of social organization. This structural parallel contributes decidedly towards confirming our observation that *-lɔdy-* refers to disputes within the community.

-gun-

In discussing this aetiological category, we rely on data from only two cases, XIII (pp. 124–5) and XXII (Appendix). The basic similarity between these two cases again lies in the categories of personnel involved. Both cases concern a member of a community in conflict with the elders. Unlike the two cases of *-lɔdy-* just discussed (which were also intra-community affairs but between individuals) the two cases of *-gun-* deal with one resident against many.

It is noteworthy that our informants' discussion of this aetiological category, unlike most of the previous ones, clearly articulated what we are suggesting is the significatum of the term. Thus, informants recognized consciously that cases of *-gun-* involve the elders of a community in conflict with a single resident.

Endasa

Data on *endasa* were difficult to gather because autopsies, which are the usual method of diagnosing this *empongo*, were curtailed during most of my stay. For a long time people feared that I was a spy for the Government. Since post-mortems by medically untrained practitioners had been outlawed under the British and were thought to be banned by the present Government as well,[1] these operations were not held in the vicinity of my home base during most of my stay. Only in the last months, when sufficient trust had developed, did three of

[1] Rumours about the Republic of Tanzania's position on autopsy circulated in Ipepete. Some said that since they now had *uhuru*, Africans could practise any of their traditional customs, including autopsy. Most of the elders continued to fear the Government, however, and were very cautious in recommending post-mortem examinations.

Aetiological Categories and the Diagnosis of Empongo

them take place. Apart from the ethnographer's presence, however, autopsy had simply declined as a routine practice through many years of government opposition, and the uncertainty over the current Government's position on the matter contributed further to this decline.

At any rate, only one of the three autopsies in our data resulted in a diagnosis of *endasa*. (Details of this instance have been reported in Cases II and III above.) Case XVI, where the diagnosis was made on a living victim, and an additional anecdote about an earlier case completes our information on diagnosed instances of this *empongo*. Although the data are thus few, they indicate certain important conclusions.

It seems significant that Mwamatete's death from *endasa* (Case III) was one of a series of such deaths deriving from a dispute between two communities which were linked through the common patrilineal descent of their headmen, since this same situation also characterized Case XVII. That case concerned a border dispute between two communities of the same tribe, although there the precise patrilineal connection between the headmen was more remote than that described in Case III. In both cases, however, instances of death by *endasa* plagued the two communities. (A more detailed description of this earlier case is provided in the Appendix, Case XVII.)

From this correspondence in the data on the two cases, a plausible inference may be drawn: *endasa* indicates a dispute between whole communities which are linked through the patrilineal tie of their headmen. The third case of *endasa* (Case XVI) supports this conclusion in that the personnel involved came from different communities of the same tribe, but I am not aware of any dispute having existed between the communities.

This inference, which posits an association between patrilineality and this manifestation of *itonga*, is consistent with the association we have observed between *-ly-* (another manifestation of *itonga*) and patrilineality. In short, *itonga* and its various manifestations (*-ly-*, *-lɔdy-*, and *endasa*) all seem to share an association with the notion of patrilineality. We shall return to this very important observation in the conclusion of this dissertation.

SUMMARY AND CONCLUSIONS

This chapter began by posing the question: what aspects of the non-linguistic environment determine the cause which will be assigned to an instance of *empongo*. Our analysis has shown that disputes in the social field become symbolized by cases of *empongo* and that the cause assigned to the *empongo* depends on the social relationship between the principal parties to the dispute signified. Thus, when the parties to the dispute are non-kinsmen of different communities, the *empongo* is attributed to medicine. When the antagonists are members of the same patrilineage, however, the cause is set down to *-ly-*. On the other hand, when the parties are non-kinsmen of the same community, the ascribed cause is *-lɔdy-* when the dispute is between individuals, and *-gun-* when an individual is involved in a disagreement with the elders of the community. Finally, when the dispute is between whole communities of the same tribe, *endasa* is the cause which is attributed to the case of *empongo* which comes to stand for the dispute. The answer to our original question, then, is clear: the determinant of the particular cause assigned to a case of *empongo* is the social relationship between the parties to a dispute which the *empongo* itself comes to stand for.

The above conclusion is not one which is consciously articulated by Safwa, although it is completely consistent with a number of other beliefs which they hold.

First, it is consistent with the belief, which we discussed in Chapter II, that disputes cause sickness and death. For, since Safwa believe that *empongo* comes from social discord, it follows logically that the various kinds of *empongo* which the Safwa recognize should refer ultimately to the discord which underlies the disease.

Second, this conclusion is consistent with beliefs overtly expressed by the Safwa concerning the causes of a number of other diseases. Thus, *ofubanye*, it will be recalled from Chapter III, is a cause of death believed to arise from an unsettled murder. The aetiology thus refers to a particular kind of dispute. Since, however, the Safwa further maintain that murder within the lineage can never cause a case of *ofubanye* and that a case of *ofubanye* has never occurred following a murder within a community, this disease also signals the social relationship between the murderer and his victim. Thus for *ofubanye* to occur, the parties concerned in a murder must be members of different lineages and residents of different communities.

Similarly *amaya* also signalizes the social relationship between parties to a dispute. It will be recalled from Chapter III that *amaya* is a condition, like complications in Western medicine, that coexists with a primary disease and is caused by a disagreement among mem-

Aetiological Categories and the Diagnosis of Empongo 109

bers of the sick person's lineage. *Amaya* thus signals a dispute between members of the same lineage. Safwa are likewise aware that *olupεmbε* too, relates to a dispute between people in a certain social relationship, in this case between non-kinsmen.

Thus, the notion that the causes of *empongo* indicate the social relationship between parties to a dispute seems characteristic of Safwa belief, although the notion itself is never generalized and is consciously articulated only for certain types of *empongo*.

An additional observation emerges from the foregoing conclusions. There is a clear contrast between the social relationships symbolized by medicines and those symbolized by manifestations of *itonga*. Medicine symbolizes disputes between non-kinsmen of different communities, people between whom no relationship of descent can be established. *Itonga*, on the other hand, symbolizes disputes between actors in those social relationships which can be conceptualized in terms of descent. Thus disputes between patrilineal kinsmen, between residents of the same community (which, as we pointed out in Chapter I, is structured and conceived by Safwa as a compound with the headman as father and compound head) and between residents of communities whose headmen are linked by a patrilineal tie all find expression in terms of *itonga*—that mysterious, unseen, inherent power. The significance of these associations between *itonga* and descent (incorporative relations) and medicines and non-kin (transactional) relationships for processes of social control among the Safwa will constitute the major concern of the following chapter.

CHAPTER V

A PRAGMATIC ANALYSIS OF THE AETIOLOGY OF EMPONGO

In this chapter we embark on a new line of analysis by asking the question: what is the effect of diagnosing a case of *empongo* in one way as opposed to another? That is, once a decision has been reached concerning the cause underlying a case of *empongo*, how does this decision influence the behaviour of the people involved?

In asking this kind of question, we are undertaking an investigation in pragmatics, 'that portion of semiotic which deals with the . . . use and effects of signs within the behaviour in which they occur' (Morris 1955:219). In the course of this investigation, we shall show that diagnosing a case of *empongo* in terms of medicines initiates a different chain of behaviour, a different set of social control mechanisms, from that which follows a diagnosis in terms of one of the several manifestations of *itonga*. We shall suggest furthermore, that the social referents of the diagnostic terms themselves are a major determinant of their different behavioural effects.

NATURE OF THE EVIDENCE

Formal and Informal Diagnoses
Formal diagnoses of *empongo* are to be understood as those arrived at through the processes of divination or autopsy, while informal diagnoses are those aired in diffuse gossip. The principal difference between the two kinds of diagnosis is that formal diagnoses, unlike rumours, represent the consensus of a clearly specifiable social group. Thus only the deceased's community attends and participates in the verdict of an autopsy, while divinations concern only members of the victim's family.[1] In contrast, rumours (although they may circulate among members of a defined social group, as Gluckman [1963] has pointed out), do not necessarily represent the consensus of such a group. Moreover, even should a group of some kind take form among

[1] For a review of the precise kinsmen who are called upon to attend a seance when someone falls ill, consult Chapter III, Table 2.

A Pragmatic Analysis of the Aetiology of Empongo 111

disparate individuals who, for one reason or another, believe the same rumour, this process of group formation represents quite a different social event from the emergence of a joint decision from a pre-existing social group in a culturally scheduled setting. The former event characterizes the birth of a faction; the latter, a regularized procedure for formulating and enunciating a group decision.

Because of this difference between formal and informal diagnoses, they are best treated separately in a pragmatic analysis. The following observations, it must be noted, rely on data from formally diagnosed cases only.

Sources of Information

Safwa usually maintain secrecy about the outcome of several kinds of divinations. First, they rarely speak of an inconclusive seance which does not produce a diagnosis upon which all the clients agree. In addition, they do not openly discuss the outcome of divinations in which certain specific causes have been diagnosed. (We shall speak of these particular divinations at greater length below.) As a result of this attitude of secrecy, it is difficult to make comprehensive statements about the effects of diagnoses of *empongo*.[2]

Rather than limit our data solely to divinations which became public, however, we managed to obtain facts about a number of secret divinations during the course of our fieldwork. To acquire this suppressed information, we used two approaches. First, we collected narratives about these divinations from close friends; and second, we approached the data through diviners as well as clients. The records of seances kept by two diviners, which are described more fully on pp. 50-1, provide pertinent data on our present problem.

These data are limited in certain respects, both in quantity and quality, however. Since there is a professional ethic of confidentiality among diviners, we could get them to keep records only by promising not to tell other Safwa about these data and by allowing our informants to preserve the anonymity of their clients by identifying them only by community of residence. As a result of these concessions, the diviners' accounts remain fragmentary in many respects because they could not be probed for further details by direct questioning of the clients. Nevertheless these accounts catalogue certain kinds of divinations, the results of which are normally kept secret and have

[2] Colson (1966: 222-3) has noted a similar attitude of secrecy following divinations among the Tonga of Zambia.

112 *Witchcraft, Sorcery, and Social Categories Among the Safwa*

consequently not found their way into most discussions of the role of divination in witchcraft and sorcery. Since we believe that this material is necessary to an understanding of the effects of divination, we are incorporating it into the following analysis. We caution the reader, however, that our conclusions are based on somewhat fragmentary material.

Frequency of Cases

To give the reader a better indication of the nature of our sample, Table VI, Column 1, presents the proportion of cases of *empongo* and barrenness in the diviners' records which fall into various diagnostic categories. The second column indicates the representation of formally diagnosed cases in our same of case histories. The discrepancy between the two distributions is due largely to the investigator's bias. Since I had greater difficulty in understanding the principles behind the meaning and use of the term *-ly-*, I collected more anecdotes about this cause of *empongo* than any other. The diviners'

TABLE VI

DIVINED CAUSES OF *EMPONGO* AND BARRENNESS: PROPORTIONS OF VARIOUS DIAGNOSES FROM DIVINERS' RECORDS AND ANECDOTAL REPORTS

	Diviners' Records (N=24)[a]	Anecdotal Reports (N = 24)
	%	%
Medicine	42	33.3
Ancestor spirits	25	—
-ly-	17	29.2
-lɔdy-	4	8.3
-tat-	4	8.3
-gun-	—	4.2
-galandy-	—	—
-las-	—	8.3
ambuda	—	4.2
No diagnosis given	8	4.2
Total	100%	100%

[a] Out of this total number of cases in the diviners' records, only 17 contain enough data to be used in the ensuing analysis. These usable cases are distributed as follows: medicine, 8; ancestor spirits, 5; *-ly-*, 4.

records undoubtedly represent a more accurate picture of the causes of *empongo* as diagnosed at that particular period of Safwa history.

It is notable that the highest proportion of cases in the diviners' records (42%) were attributed to medicines. Since this diagnostic category implies a dispute among parties of different communities, it suggests that disharmony is ascribed most frequently to social relationships involving the least interaction. In other words, clients at seances apparently tend to see *empongo* as inflicted by agents outside the network of people with whom they interact most frequently. The reasons for this fact will become apparent below.

With this preliminary description of the data out of the way, we now enter into the analysis of the effects of diagnoses phrased in terms of both *itonga* and medicines. The aim of this analysis is to show the contrast between the effects of these two kinds of diagnosis and to indicate the role of the concepts of *itonga* and medicine in producing these contrasting effects.

THE USES AND EFFECTS OF FORMAL DIAGNOSES
IN TERMS OF *ITONGA*

It will be remembered from Chapter III that -*ly*-, -*lɔdy*-, *endasa*, and -*gun*- are aetiological categories which all trace their origin to the unseen power of *itonga*. At the conclusion of the last chapter we noted the association of all these terms with groups which express their unity in an idiom of agnatic descent. The following discussion shows that the introduction of diagnoses of *itonga* into a dispute situation points up this status relationship between the antagonists. Since the highest value of patrilineal kinship is unity (being of 'one heart'), emphasis on the patrilineal tie brings this ethic into prominence in the dispute. As a result, one of the major effects of diagnoses of *itonga* is efforts at reconciliation of the parties; failing this, after a period in which the antagonists vie with one another to demonstrate support for their own position, a break in the patrilineal tie occurs. Our main point is that this range of effects depends on the importance of the patrilineal tie in the conception of this dispute, and this importance is introduced, in turn, by the diagnosis of *itonga*.

The Effects of a Diagnosis of -ly-

If a divination results in a diagnosis of -*ly*-, the clients—as we have shown in the previous chapter—are saying that there is someone within the patrilineage who does not co-operate, who is diminishing the personnel of the lineage. Thus a divination of -*ly*- at a seance immediately places the underlying dispute in the context of the patrilineal relationship. From that point, the effects of the divination are either to preserve the relationship or ultimately to sever it. The first means of attempting a reconciliation is the convocation of a second divination.

The Second Divination
In some instances a diviner and his clients will agree not only on a diagnosis of -*ly*- but also on the name of the kinsman involved in such approbrious behaviour. If the kinsman is named, then a second divination is arranged and the supposed culprit is invited to attend. He is not told, however, that he is suspected of having inflicted *empongo* on the victim; he is simply informed that his attendance is requested at a seance for a member of his patrilineage. (This procedure is exemplified in Case VI, Incident 1.)

Since a person is considered obligated to attend a seance only when requested to do so by either his headman or an agnatic kinsman, an agnate's response to this kind of request becomes a test both of his commitment to lineage unity ('one-heartedness') and of the first divination. Thus, if the presumed culprit appears amicably at the divination, it shows that he *is* concerned about the affairs of his patrilineage and therefore that the delinquency implied in the first divination was only a temporary lapse. If, however, he either fails to appear or reacts angrily at the seance, the suspicions expressed in the original divination are vindicated.

Days of the Ordeal. In the past, second divinations involved subjecting the assembled members of the patrilineage to an ordeal in order to determine who among them was consuming his fellows. This ordeal involved administering to all suspects a concoction made from the bark of a tree (*ɔmwavi*). If a suspect vomited the *ɔmwavi*, he was considered innocent. If he retained it, he became bloated but was then given an antidote if he acknowledged his anti-social behaviour. Only if he refused to admit his culpability after all these opportunities to confess, was he reportedly killed. In instances where more than one member of the patrilineage retained the concoction, all the afflicted members were considered to have been involved in a mutual struggle to consume one another.

Because the ordeal was outlawed by the British and has therefore

A Pragmatic Analysis of the Aetiology of Empongo

not been administered (so far as I was able to determine) since the 1930s, it is extremely difficult to assess these reports about its use. First of all, they give no clue about the frequency with which the ordeal was actually administered. Furthermore, while informants today recall that ɔmwavi was not applicable in all circumstances, they are unable to verbalize the precise conditions which differentiated applicable from inapplicable cases. There is complete agreement, however, that ɔmwavi was administered at seances. Since we have pointed out that one need attend only seances called by one's headman or patrilineal kin, ɔmwavi was thus administered only in the presence of people who shared some kind of patrilineal bond.

The main conclusion one reaches from these data, however, is that the ordeal was used less with the intention of testing culpability than of eliciting a confession and providing a situation in which a suspect could demonstrate his unity with his patrilineal kin and thus effect a reconciliation among them.

Contemporary Effects of Divinations

Unlike accounts from the days of the ɔmwavi ordeal, the contemporary effects of diagnoses of -ly- are somewhat easier to assess. We can distinguish three such effects: (1) reconciliation of the disputants, (2) severance of the patrilineal tie between disputants, and (3) public tests of support by the disputants. As we shall show, each of these effects gains meaning only through recognition of the patrilineal ethic of unity, which is introduced into the situation by the diagnosis of *itonga*.

Diagnoses Leading to Reconciliation. Today, as in the past, suspected patrilineal kinsmen are called to a second seance, but now open discussion of the conflict situation has replaced the ordeal. It is difficult to estimate the actual proportion of these second seances which conclude in harmony, since divinations which implicate a co-member of one's patrilineage are never discussed in public. The diviners' records supply our only clue to this proportion.

Of the four diagnoses of -ly- in this sample, three resulted in a second seance before the same diviner. At the conclusion of the second seance in one of these cases, the protagonists agreed to perform rites to their ancestors to show that they were 'of one heart'. In one of the other two cases a reconciliation was also arranged but without the performance of a special rite. Thus, 50% of the diagnosed cases eventuated in ostensible resolution of conflict and mollification of ill feeling.

116 *Witchcraft, Sorcery, and Social Categories Among the Safwa*

The following case history, recounted by an Ipepete informant, also indicates the revitalization of a feeling of 'one heart' after a seance prompted by a diagnosis of *-ly-*.

Case XI

There were three brothers in Ipepete—Mamɛngɛ, Empola, and Ndɛni. Ndɛni confided to me that in the past there had been bad feeling between his two older brothers. The source of this ill will was the division of their father's *eshiipa*. Mamɛngɛ, as the oldest brother, had been charged with this duty. Since Empola was serving as a conscript in World War II at the time his father died, he felt that he had not been consulted about the disposal of the gardens. According to Ndɛni, however, Mamɛngɛ had kept the estate intact until Empola's return. From what I could establish, the disagreement centred around two fields in particular.

Mamɛngɛ suffered from coughing spells and consulted a diviner about them. He was told that his brothers were jealous of him. At first he was given a medicine to rub on his face as protection against this, but when the symptoms continued, the diviner concluded that one of the brothers was consuming Mamɛngɛ's vitals (*-ly-*). The brothers went together to the diviner, and there Empola confessed his anger against his brother. The reasons for the anger were discussed and settlement was reached about the fields. Ndɛni claimed that since that time, 'We are of one heart.'

Thus, perhaps half the diagnoses of *-ly-* result in the reconciliation of disputing parties today. Moreover, this reconciliation is phrased in terms of a return to one heart, the patrilineal ethic. It is significant that these diagnoses are kept secret: dissension within a patrilineage should not be aired outside it if, in the upshot, the members are of 'one heart'. Indeed not even the headman need be informed when members of a patrilineage consult a diviner about a possible case of *-ly-* among them, nor need they inform him of the result of such a divination. It is undoubtedly this pressure towards secrecy which accounts for the infrequence (only one case out of nine) with which cases of *-ly-* that reached settlement are reported in our anecdotal record.

It is relevant to note here that diagnoses either of *amaya* or of the complicity of the ancestors in an instance of disease or death guarantee a public expression of reconciliation by necessitating an ancestor rite to effect a cure. In the previous chapter we called attention to the

A Pragmatic Analysis of the Aetiology of Empongo

superadded quality of these two aetiological categories. We now see that these categories may in fact be appended to other diagnoses to help bring about a public demonstration of unanimity in a patrilineage.

Diagnoses Leading to Lineage Fission. Perhaps the most dramatic result of some diagnoses of *-ly-* is the ultimate avoidance of social contacts, leading to fission of the lineage. Although none of our diviners' cases eventuated in this way, the following case from Ipepete recounts an outcome of this sort.

Case XII

Mwankoshi and Mwangonela were brothers from different houses, who lived around the turn of the century. Although both were headmen, Mwankoshi, being the offspring of the first house, had greater authority than his brother. Mwangonela is said to have been jealous and began to consume (*-ly-*) several of Mwankoshi's children. The matter was brought before a diviner and the poison ordeal showed that Mwangonela was guilty. Although he confessed and was thus spared, Mwankoshi burned his compound and those of all his followers. He drove them away, and all contact between the two segments was severed for two generations. After this time a descendant of Mwangonela brought his family back to Ipepete to live, and the lineal bond was re-established.

Several stories like this one were known and told in Ipepete, almost always in the past tense before the time the poison ordeal was outlawed. A diagnosis of *-ly-* which occurred after the abandonment of the *ɔmwavi* ordeal and led to lineage fission, however, was that between Ontewa and Mwanzumba (Case VIII, p. 98). In this case Mwanzumba had disregarded several invitations to divinations for Ontewa's children, but it was not until Mwanzumba was charged with the death of the headman's son that a breach between the two brothers occurred formally. It would appear, therefore, that Ontewa needed the backing of the headman and other elders before he could initiate the break with Mwanzumba. Not until Mwanzumba was seen as attacking the community itself by consuming a son of the headman, the symbol of the community, did Ontewa command the support necessary to oust his brother.

In short, the severance of an incorporative (patrilineal) tie was accomplished after a diagnosis of *-ly-*, but only with community involvement as well. In Case VIII this involvement was elicited by a divination in which the offending kinsman was made responsible for the death of a member of the headman's family. In Case XII community involvement (which was certainly necessary for Mwankoshi to have ousted not only his brother but 'all his people' as well, to quote our informants' account) was elicited by the verdict of the ordeal. Although there are important differences between these two cases (viz. one took place before the abolition of the *ɔmwavi* ordeal, the second after; one involved the chiefly patrilineage, the other only commoners) the fact that the community became involved in both cases constitutes a striking similarity.

In this respect, therefore, a notable contrast exists between cases of -*ly*- which lead to reconciliation within the lineage and those which lead to fission. On the one hand, cases which lead to reconciliation definitely do not involve the community. (In fact, as we have seen, there are tabus against even speaking of these cases within the community.) On the other hand, cases which result in lineage fission do involve members of the community. Given this contrast, we might expect an interim effect of diagnoses of -*ly*- to be a situation in which the protagonists vie with one another for supporters within the community. We consider this effect next.

Diagnoses Leading to Public Tests of Support. Although two of the cases in the diviners' records led to results of this sort, Case VI from our anecdotal data provides a more detailed instance. In that case Ntandala's asthma was attributed by divination to -*ly*-. Since Mwakingili refused to accompany Ntandala to any subsequent divination, the disagreement between them remained unsettled. Yet it did not lead to an open break between them, either. Instead, the dispute became public and was aired periodically—once at the death of Mwakingili's mother, again at a meeting of headmen to pray for the cessation of rain, again at the hearing following the name-calling incident, and still again at the meeting convoked as a result of an epidemic among children.

This publicity converted the dispute from a private estrangement between brothers into a public test of power between them. Indeed, the hearing which Ntandala called in response to Mwakingili's alleged insult was little more than a demonstration of his own power. By attesting that Mwakingili had uttered the slight, the witnesses publicly proclaimed their alignment with Ntandala.

This was only one of a series of such public displays of support, however. A similar occasion had arisen several months before that,

A Pragmatic Analysis of the Aetiology of Empongo

when Ntandala held an ancestor ceremony at his parents' graves. This ceremony was marked by the sacrifice of a special bull in order to mollify the ancestors' anger over the improper burial of the son of one of Ntandala's and Mwakingili's half-brothers.[3] The fact that the half-brother sacrificed at Ntandala's rites publicized the friendship and alliance between these two. Many residents of the brothers' community who attended the rites also expressed support for Ntandala by their very presence at this assembly and not at an *omwɛngulɔ* ceremony held by Mwakingili about a month before.

That ceremony, in honour of Mwakingili's and Kabɛta's mother, had been an opportunity for people to show their alignment with Mwakingili. Since he and Kabɛta—who was Ntandala's ally (see pp. 94–6 again for details)—held separate but simultaneous rites, attendance at one of these rites to the exclusion of the other was an expression of support for the host.

Rather than taking sides publicly with either antagonist, however, many people attended all these ceremonies indiscriminately. For these people, who chose to remain uncommitted to one brother or the other, a knowledge of the dispute was nonetheless essential in enabling them to act appropriately neutral on all these kinds of occasions.

For Ntandala himself the public dispute was more than a mere test of power with his brother. For him a greater political gain was at stake: his acceptance into the chiefly lineage. So long as this dispute continued to promote factionalism in his home community of Mabandɛ, there was a possibility that the headmen of other neighbouring communities might intervene. And, as we pointed out above, such intervention would have supported his claim to membership in the chiefly lineage, since the only ground upon which headmen of other communities may customarily intervene is common descent.

The early onset of the rainy season in 1963 provided an event which almost brought about this intervention. Since an unexpected deviation from the normal rainfall pattern is believed to be caused by the anger of the chiefly ancestor spirits, and this anger is evoked primarily by wrangling in their homeland, the early rains led the living members of Mwanabantu lineage to try to stop any disputes in the land. As a result, a meeting of all headmen in Magombɛ was convened in the sacred grove at Ipepete in order to stop dissension and thereby hold back the rains.

[3] The son had died while working on a sisal estate in Northern Tanzania and had been buried there, instead of at home as custom required.

At this meeting the behaviour of those who were 'spoiling' Mabande community was discussed at some length. The discussion concluded, however, with the phrase, 'It is a matter for their own community (*empaŋa*),' the very statement which called a halt to discussions of this issue at the public meeting held several months later in response to the epidemic among children. This repeated statement by members of the chiefly lineage served two purposes: (1) it helped contain the dispute within the brothers' patrilineage, and (2) by inhibiting involvement of headmen in the quarrel, it frustrated Ntandala's hope of recognition as a member of the chiefly lineage.

In sum, when the dispute became public, it thereby became a focus for power politics. Both Ntandala and Mwakingili held ceremonies which enabled them to demonstrate their backing. In addition, Ntandala exploited the situation to further his personal goal of full acceptance into the chiefly lineage. On the other hand, those not directly involved in the dispute could use the public knowledge of its existence to regulate their own behaviour in terms of the power struggle, taking sides or not as they chose. Since our data, as we observed above, show that the community becomes involved in an intra-lineage dispute before fission occurs, both Ntandala and Mwakingili seem to have been building support for such a break. No break occurred during our stay in the field, however, and the efforts of other headmen to contain the dispute within the lineage seem to have been responsible for this.

It is important to note that the ambiguous valuation of the power of *itonga*—the belief that it can be used for both philanthropic and misanthropic ends—is related to its use in these political circumstances, since it allows groups to polarize around their evaluation of the use of this power.

Summary: Diagnoses of -ly-
What these data suggest is that a diagnosis of -*ly*- phrases a dispute squarely in terms of the agnatic status relationship between the antagonists. By this means the possible outcomes of the dispute become regulated by the values of that status relationship, specifically its ethic of unity. The disputants are thus faced with the alternative of either reconciling their difference or severing the relationship altogether, an act which apparently requires public support from outside before it will be consummated. The influence of the ethic of patrilineal unity on the outcomes of diagnoses in terms of the remain-

A Pragmatic Analysis of the Aetiology of Empongo   121

ing manifestations of *itonga* will become apparent in the following discussion.

The Effects of a Diagnosis of Endasa

Endasa, it will be recalled, is a mortal affliction of people who possess the power of *itonga*. It results from their being 'speared' during nocturnal battles with other possessors of this power. Our data on instances of *endasa* consist of three anecdotal cases: two (Cases III and XVI), which occurred during my field stay, and the other (Case XVII), which occurred approximately twenty years ago. All three cases involved personnel from two communities linked by the patrilineal tie of their headmen. In Cases III and XVII the two communities were embroiled in a long dispute, and diagnoses of *endasa* placed the disputes clearly within the context of the patrilineal ethic.

In Case III (the one which the writer witnessed), a conflict had arisen when people from Igamba community planted gardens claimed by residents of Ibala community. The initial instances of *endasa* which were associated with this conflict had all been interpreted as the aftermath of the nocturnal battles between the defenders of both communities. The case of *endasa* which was diagnosed while I was in the field, however, was construed instead as arising from the repayment of blood debts which had been incurred by the defenders of the aggressor community during the forementioned conflict. Thus, from an interpretation which viewed deaths in the community as externally induced, the new interpretation moved to an explanation in terms of an internal cause. This change was almost immediately followed by the scheduling of an ancestor rite for the common forebear of the headmen of the two communities—i.e. the confirmation of the patrilineal tie.

The rationale behind this sudden desire on the part of former enemies to come together in a rite which would formally announce the termination of this dispute was the aggressor community's belief (expressed in the diagnosis of *endasa*) that the conflict had resulted in their own defenders' having killed a fellow resident. In their own eyes the dispute had become, in short, self-defeating. People spoke of the need for members of both communities to pray together to the chiefly ancestors in order to enlist their protection against the blood creditors to which each of their defenders had become indebted during the conflict. In this opposition between communities within the same tribe, the diagnosis of *endasa*, by keeping the status relationship between the two communities in the forefront of the dispute, led to a reconciliation between them on the basis of their common patrilineality. At the time I left the field, a bull was being sought to sacrifice at this important ancestor ceremony.

Although Case XVII involves *endasa* and is remarkably similar to the foregoing one in many ways, Government intervention seems ultimately to have produced a different result. Case XVII also involved a land dispute (in this case over boundaries), which generated diagnoses of *endasa* in the two communities involved. These diagnoses repeatedly attributed the cause of death to nocturnal attacks by defenders of the rival community. Thus far, our two cases are similar.

Since one of the headmen involved in this case was the British-appointed Chief of the Safwa, however, the dispute attained particular importance in the eyes of the authorities. For this reason—and the added one that the Chief, already experienced in Western judicial procedures and notions of evidence, had little to fear from a Government investigation—the dispute reached the courts. The verdict of the court honoured the Chief's claims and declared the rival community to be trespassers on his land. This decision, which was taken by the protagonists as confirmation of the Chief's triumph in the nightly battle of the defenders, effectively put an end to the dispute.

Unlike the previous cases which took place entirely within the idiom of *itonga*, the losers in this case were presented with a *fait accompli* by the Government. They were not given the opportunity to reassess the situation in their own time and come to their own decision to drop the dispute and bury hard feelings. Although the diagnosis of *endasa* linked the dispute to patrilineal ideology, Government intervention deprived the losers of their own way of reaching the decision to capitulate and, more important, of expressing this capitulation in the idiom of patrilineal unity. As a result, no lasting *rapprochement* between the two communities has ever emerged. Today the losers in some years refuse to attend the annual ancestor rites entirely; in other years they come only to argue the old issue at their forebears' gravesides.

We conclude from these two cases that incidents of *endasa* can help precipitate a reconciliation between whole communities of the same tribe which are locked in a dispute. We suggest that they do this by always raising the dispute in the context of the patrilineal status relationship between the disputing parties and thereby providing the disputants with the symbolic means of effecting a reconciliation when external conditions are propitious.

The Effects of a Diagnosis of -lɔdy-

Since the data from the diviners' records on this aetiological category are too fragmentary to include in our data, our present analysis is limited to Cases IX and X. The first of these cases, which concerned Mwanaŋwa's dispute over a field belonging to his fellow resident in Ipepete community, Mwasapile, became a political issue while we were in the field. Consequently, Case X, which involved the marriage of Mwanaŋwa's son Yacɔbɔ to the headman's daughter, provided an opportunity for residents of Ipepete to express their feelings about Mwanaŋwa. This was done in two ways: first, by rumours and second, by the decision expressed at the moot following Wambe's elopement.

Some rumours which circulated in Ipepete at the time stated that various people in the community were making Wambe ill in order to prevent her from marrying Yacɔbɔ; these rumours came from supporters of Mwanaŋwa. On the other hand, those who sided with Mwasapile's kinsmen countered with the rumour that Mwanaŋwa himself was causing the girl's illness. (See Incident 2 of this case.)

Wambe herself stepped into this political arena and, taking advantage of Mwanaŋwa's precarious position in the community, broke off her marriage with his son. The case of her elopement with another lad of the community was thus heard by the elders, a procedure upon which the headman himself insisted for fear of being suspected of having arranged the elopement himself in order to terminate the marriage. The overwhelming consensus of this hearing was that Wambe should not return to Yacɔbɔ. Since the bulk of the bridewealth had already been paid, this rather unusual decision was indicative of the community's feelings regarding their headman's consummating a marital alliance with Mwanaŋwa. During most of our field stay Mwanaŋwa remained a social isolate except for his weekly appearance to participate in the agricultural tasks on the community's common fields.

These two related cases demonstrate a number of things. First, as the hearing about the field indicates, there is a tendency to try to settle disputes within the community initially by judicial means. Only after reconciliation failed to take place by that means, did recourse to the idiom of *empongo* occur. While not a surprising phenomenon, a second observation which these cases suggest is that when disputes become open to public scrutiny and debates, they may be used by individuals to further their own ends. Thus Wambe used Mwanaŋwa's reputation to justify her refusal to marry his son. We witnessed a similar phenomenon in Case VI, when Ntandala used his dispute with his brother as a means of furthering his own goal of full acceptance into Mwanabantu lineage. Thus, once a dispute has been symbolized in terms of one of the causes of *empongo* and the matter then opened to public debate, individuals may use the situation to further their own ends.

Finally, symbolizing the dispute in Case IX in terms of *-lɔdy-* resulted in procedures similar to those which follow a diagnosis of *-ly-*. Thus the marriage of Mwanaŋwa's son provided the community with an occasion for enunciating their opinions of Mwanaŋwa, just as public expressions of support for the antagonists characterize the aftermath of diagnoses of *-ly-*.

The Effects of a Diagnosis of -gun-

The following is the only formally diagnosed case of *-gun-* in our data. (Case XXII, although it concerns *-gun-*, was not formally diagnosed.)

Case XIII

Mayoni was a disagreeable middle-aged man who was frequently involved in petty disputes with members of his community. These disputes led to a pervasive feeling of ill will against him in the community, and his main defence against this was to try to become indispensable to the headman. To begin with, he was the headman's maternal uncle, and he conspicuously displayed signs of good *itonga* on his nephew's behalf. Thus he was said to have threatened a member of another community, with whom his nephew was not on good terms, by saying 'The men of our community will see to you.' (The 'men' in this threat being the men of *itonga*.)

In the mid-1950s Mayoni developed a swelling in his arm which did not go away on application of the usual remedies. He began suggesting that various people in the community were responsible for his affliction, although he had not consulted a diviner about it. The headman pressured him into seeing a diviner, who diagnosed his condition as *-gun-*. In other words, men of *itonga* in the community were collectively causing his affliction as punishment.

Mayoni reported the divination to the headman, who called a meeting of all the elders of Isoko. They talked over their differences with Mayoni, who, it was reported, appeared at the meeting very contrite and apologetic (as befitted a meeting of this sort). Mayoni promised to reform his ways and killed a goat for all to eat together as a sign of his reunion with the community.

When I asked Mayoni about this incident, he gave another reason why the *abitonga* of Isoko had inflicted the swollen arm on him. He claimed that they were jealous of his close relationship with the headman.

Commentary on Case XIII. The parallel between the results of this case and the results of cases involving diagnoses of *-ly-* is indeed striking. Thus, symbolizing the disaffection towards Mayoni in terms of *-gun-* brought about a meeting of the elders where ill-feelings and grudges were aired, much as diagnoses of *-ly-* produce second seances where members of the patrilineage air their differences. Furthermore, just as these seances can reconcile members of the patrilineage, so the meeting with Mayoni proved successful in reconciling him with the community. The one diagnosed case of *-gun-* in our records thus suggests that this aetiological category sets in motion similar events to a diagnosis of *-ly-*.

Conclusions: The Effects of Diagnoses in Terms of Itonga

We have seen that disputes which become symbolized as cases of *-ly-* may proceed towards any of three states: reconciliation of the disputants, severance of the patrilineal tie between disputants, or public displays of support for the individual disputants. Since the diagnosis of *-ly-* is a constant in each of these outcomes, we cannot explain the variety of outcomes by the constant. However, we suggest that these outcomes constitute a range of effects induced by symbolizing a dispute in terms of *-ly-*. Our contrast of the effects of diagnoses of *itonga* with the effects of diagnoses of medicines in the next section will show this to be in fact true. For the present, however, we are simply suggesting that association of the dispute with *-ly-* is the cause of these effects.

Our data on the other manifestations of *itonga* suggest that they, too, eventuate in the same three outcomes. We therefore feel justified in generalizing the foregoing suggestion to all aetiological categories pertaining to *itonga*. In short, we conclude that symbolizing a dispute in terms of *itonga* confines the outcome of the dispute within the circumscribed range of possibilities described above.

We submit that this is so because the concept of *itonga* (which, as we saw in the previous chapter, indicates that the parties to a dispute are connected by a patrilineal bond) places the conflict over material goods or some other substantive issue within the context of a patrilineal (incorporative) status relationship. The various terms of the aetiological system convey two bits of information—(1) there is a dispute, and (2) the protagonists are agnates—rather than just the one bit conveyed by outright discussions of the disagreement. Once this nexus between the dispute and patrilineality has been established, the value of unity—the core concept of the lineal ideology—can be used to help induce settlement of the dispute.

We furthermore suggest that this procedure of accusation in terms of *itonga* is necessary precisely because of the vagueness of the norms specifying one's obligation to one's lineal kin, a feature we noted in Chapter I. These obligations are expressed in terms of 'being of one heart'. Moreover, the rules specifying the obligations which one must meet in order to comply with this injunction are broad. As we saw in Chapter II, the precise activities which constitute instances of spoiling (*-nandy-*) or weakening (*-tul-*) social bonds are often unclearly defined. As a result, a particular instance of rule-breaking or belligerence may be considered a violation of lineage ethics by some members and not by others. However, by allowing a dispute to become symbolized as a manifestation of *itonga* in the course of a divination, the clients make the connection between a particular dispute and the patrilineal status relationship—in short, define the activity as a violation of patrilineal ethics.

Once this is done, the culprit becomes subject to the sanctions of the patrilineal status. He must then either demonstrate that he is 'of one heart' with his lineage or ultimately deny the patrilineal tie altogether. We have seen that these two alternatives form the opposite poles of response to a diagnosis of *-ly-*, with manipulation for support as the intervening response. Our data on the other manifestations of *itonga* suggest that this is true for them as well.

Which one of the three responses will actually follow a diagnosis of

A Pragmatic Analysis of the Aetiology of Empongo

itonga is undoubtedly explained by ecological, demographic, economic and political conditions. We unfortunately do not possess these in sufficient detail to explain this part of the process. Collection of these data therefore remains an important task for future research.

THE USES AND EFFECTS OF FORMAL DIAGNOSES IN TERMS OF MEDICINES

We can confirm the above conclusions by contrasting the aforementioned effects of diagnoses in terms of the manifestations of *itonga* with the effects of diagnoses phrased in terms of medicines. Since, as we concluded in the previous chapter, medicines entail a different status relationship from manifestations of *itonga*, we would expect that disputes which are symbolized in these terms should display a different range of outcomes from those diagnosed as *itonga*. Furthermore, we would expect the outcomes to accord with the norms of the non-kin (transactional) relationship implied by this aetiological term. Let us examine the effects of diagnoses of medicine with these hypotheses in mind.

In discussing the effects of diagnoses of *empongo* phrased in terms of medicine, we are on somewhat firmer ground than in the previous section because of the larger number of cases in our sample. For this analysis we have eight cases in the records of the two diviners and eight from our own case histories.

Cases of *empongo* attributed to medicines may differ subtly in their precise aetiology, and it will profit us to review the differences briefly before beginning our analysis. Medicines, it will be remembered, work in conjunction with the life forces in a situation to produce their effect, and it is this contingent causality which lends subtlety to concepts about the workings of medicines.

The most direct causal connection between medicine and *empongo* is exemplified by medicines which have been concocted for the particular purpose of producing the diminution of a specific life force. (See, for example, Case VII, pp. 97–8 or Case XXI in the Appendix). Medicines of this type, however, are also believed capable of rebounding on a kinsman of the procurer, if the latter's vital force is less than that of the intended victim. (The Jumbe's divination in Case II illustrates this aetiology.) A variant of this cause of *empongo* is exemplified by Case IV, in which a medicine rebounded upon a member of the procurer's lineage through the power, not of the intended victim, but rather of the medicine man who prepared it. A final possibility in this range of causes is for a medicine, procured to enhance the vital force of its possessor, to react adversely upon members of either the lineage or community to which he belongs.

Although these diagnostic alternatives are all similar in attributing *empongo* to medicine, they obviously differ from one another with regard to: (1) the social relationship between the victim and the possessor of the medicine and/or (2) the assignment of culpability. This very variety of ways in which medicines are believed to cause *empongo* has an important bearing on their effects, as we shall see.

Essentially there are two courses of action open to people who have received a divination in terms of medicine. By far the most common procedure is for the victim simply to protect himself against further *empongo* by acquiring more potent medicines. The other alternative is to attempt some kind of settlement of the underlying dispute, in addition to obtaining a medicine to enhance one's vital force. We shall consider these alternatives in turn.

Diagnoses Leading Only to the Acquisition of More Medicines
In examining this result of cases of medicinally caused *empongo* the investigator is once more faced with the problem of secrecy. If a victim simply acquires a medicine to combat the debilitating effects of his *empongo*, usually nothing is ever said about the diagnosis. Indeed it is generally believed that if, on the basis of a divination, one publicly accuses the person named of possessing a medicine, the accuser will be stricken instantly. Only a diviner or other person with a great deal of vital force is believed capable of making such an accusation.

Sometimes, however, a diagnosis in terms of medicines does become public, but this usually happens only a considerable time after the divination has taken place. This public revelation often occurs in the following way. Since a victim of any *empongo* always obtains a medicine as a cure, this same medicine may later be used as an explanation for an attack of *empongo* among the kin of the supposed holder of the original medicine. Since the effect of the curing medicine will not come to light until the case of retaliatory *empongo* occurs, the time which elapses before anything is said publicly about the original case may thus be considerable.

Indeed a good many cases of this nature seem to remain permanently under wraps. Our field notes contain numerous anecdotes,

A Pragmatic Analysis of the Aetiology of Empongo 129

collected confidentially in Ipepete, about divinations in terms of medicines which never entered the public domain.[4] In addition, of the five cases in the diviners' records which occurred in June and October 1963 (eight and four months respectively before we left the field), the formal interpretation of only one of these cases had become public before our departure.[5] These data thus suggest that when the close kin of a victim accept a divination in terms of medicines, they tend to keep the matter secret and combat it by medicinal means. It is as if the failure to act reciprocally in normal social contexts, which lies at the root of most disputes between non-kinsmen, were replaced by reciprocal activity, in secret, with medicines.

The parallel between the normal, open mode of interaction between non-kinsmen and this hostile, secret mode is indeed striking. We remember that normally non-kinsmen interact in an idiom of strict reciprocity. The mutual stockpiling of medicines by antagonists, in order to equalize their vital forces, duplicates this reciprocal mode of behaviour. Thus, when a supposed victim of medicinal attack falls ill, he obtains a medicine to counter the one which is thought to be making him ill; when his nemesis in turn falls ill, he in turn obtains an additional medicine to overcome his now obviously stronger victim. The reciprocal behaviour of the non-kin relationship is clearly repeated through medicines.

Indeed one might even say that using medicines is not deviant behaviour in the same way in which the use of *itonga* can be deviant. When a family accepts a divination in terms of *-ly-*, for example, they are saying that a member of the patrilineage is behaving in a manner which is detrimental to the unity of the group and thus in violation of this ideal norm of the patrilineage. This is expressed symbolically by saying that the villain is diminishing the strength of the group by consuming the vitals of one or more of its members. On the other hand, when a family accepts a divination in terms of medicine, they are saying that a non-kinsman is reducing the vital force of one of their members. By then procuring a counter-medicine, they are acting

---

[4] These anecdotes are not included in the record of cases presented in the body of this dissertation or in the Appendix because the underlying disputes were often not clearly specified. Our information on them consists simply of statements that when a particular person was ill, the diviner diagnosed the cause as a medicine.

[5] Of the eight diagnoses of medicines in the diviners' records, seven fall under this category of instances which were followed only by the accumulation of more medicines. We have omitted two of these cases from consideration in this generalization because they were diagnosed in February 1964, only a few weeks before we left the field. There was thus insufficient time for them to have become public.

within the pattern of the reciprocal mode of behaviour which characterizes social relations between non-kin. It is perhaps this conformity between the behaviour concerning medicines and the usual social patterns between non-kinsmen that leads Safwa to consider medicines comprehensible and non-mysterious in contra-distinction to *itonga*, which, as we pointed out in Chapter III, is somehow incomprehensible and mysterious.

Diagnoses Resulting in Attempts at Reconciliation
After a divination in which someone from another community has been implicated in a case of *empongo*, that person may be approached by kinsmen of the victim in order to attempt settling any underlying dissension. At such a meeting the person implicated is never accused of causing *empongo* through medicine. Instead, the approach is made entirely in terms of the real dispute.

Cases IV, VII, and XIV (see Appendix) in our Ipepete data all exemplify attempts at reconciliation following a diagnosis of *empongo* in terms of medicine. One case out of eight from the diviners' records also followed this course.

Significantly, in every one of the cases in which a reconciliation was attempted, the aetiology identified a patrilineal kinsman of the victim as holder of the medicine. Thus, in Case IV, a brother of the deceased held a medicine which had supposedly been turned against his lineage by the practitioner who had concocted it. In the two remaining cases, however, the medicine was believed to have been procured by the kinsman specifically to harm the victim. In Case VII this was done by the victim's brother; and in Case XIV presumably by the victim's father, although her classificatory mother was also implicated. (We shall discuss this very informative case shortly.) In the one case of this type from the diviners' records, the medicine was held by the victim's classificatory father.

Out of these four cases, only one (Case XIV) resulted in even a partial settlement of the issues between the antagonists. The remaining three cases led to no apparent settlement. Nevertheless the association of an attempt at reconciliation with a patrilineal tie between the holder of the medicine and the victim is noteworthy. Thus, even though a dispute may be between non-kinsmen and therefore symbolized in terms of medicines, the particular phrasing of the case may elicit an attempt at reconciliation through assigning possession of the medicine to a patrilineal kinsman of the victim.

A Pragmatic Analysis of the Aetiology of Empongo

The peculiar force of the patrilineal tie in fostering reconciliation is dramatically revealed in Case XIV. There Sɛlela's infertility was attributed to a medicine, and the diviner indicated that the girl's mother and father were both angry. Yet a reconciliation was effected only with her father, the patrilineal kinsman. Although great concern was shown over the anger of the mother and her second husband, significantly no settlement of the cause of their anger took place.

Case IV suggests some additional interesting observations about the dynamics of diagnoses in terms of medicines in relation to the patrilineal tie. It will be remembered that this case involved a petty diviner, Mlɔzi, who had procured a medicine for an unknown purpose from a diviner in another community. When afterward several members of Mlɔzi's lineage died, divination attributed the cause to this medicine, which had supposedly been redirected by the diviner against Mlɔzi's lineage because he had never paid for it. After three of Mlɔzi's kinsmen had reportedly died from the medicine, the Chief, exploiting the power vested in him by his Government appointment, tried unsuccessfully to arrange a compromise over payment of the debt.

With the passage of time, more members of Mlɔzi's lineage died. Finally the divination prompted by the death of his sister, which occurred while we were in the field, not only echoed the message of previous divinations but also stated that Mlɔzi was not a proper diviner and used his power of *itonga* to kill people who consulted him. To say in this way that Mlɔzi had bad *itonga* in front of members of his own lineage suggested the possibility of his using this *itonga* to consume (*-ly-*) his patrilineal kinsmen as well.

Thus, although this divination agreed in substance with prior divinations, it left the way open to change the diagnosis of subsequent cases of *empongo* in Mlɔzi's lineage from medicine to *-ly-*. That is, it provided the ideology for perceiving future *empongo* among Mlɔzi's patrilineal kinsmen as the result, no longer of his negligence in a contractual arrangement with an outsider, but as due to an act of direct aggression on his part.

Indeed, this redefinition of the situation in the vocabulary of disease aetiology paralleled the *de facto* social situation, where the focus of attention was shifting from Mlɔzi's dispute with the alien diviner to the devastation he was wreaking on his own lineage. In local gossip the issue of greatest concern was no longer Mlɔzi's debt *per se*, but his consistent failure to pay this debt and the consequent death of his patrilineal kinsmen in the vicinity. People began to suggest that, in failing to pay the debt, Mlɔzi was wilfully killing members of his own lineage. In short, from a dispute between Mlɔzi and his creditor, the issue was becoming one between Mlɔzi and his lineage.

The logic behind this shift was provided by symbolization of the dispute in terms of *empongo*. That is, by originally symbolizing Mlɔzi's delinquency in terms of a medicine which was decimating his lineage, the lineage itself became involved in a matter which was initially Mlɔzi's private concern. When he then neglected his obligation towards his creditor and permitted the medicine to continue its vicious effects, he thereby violated the ethic of lineage unity ('one heart'). This turn of events then became expressed in the ideology of *empongo* by a divination which invested him with bad *itonga*. Thus, the symbolism of *empongo* served first to involve members of Mlɔzi's lineage in what was essentially a private dispute between him and the diviner, and then permitted the dispute with an outsider to be reinterpreted as an abuse of lineage ethics.

Whether or not this reinterpretation ever brought about a settlement of the underlying dispute, however, is problematic. Unfortunately we did not have an opportunity to observe the effects of the new interpretation, since it emerged only a few months before our departure from the field. As a portent of future developments, however, it is significant that Mlɔzi openly vowed never to use his *itonga* for evil purposes again—a fact which he willingly related to me, although he still remained evasive about the outcome of the meeting with his creditor. (See account of this case, p. 91.) In doing this, he was obviously more concerned to dispel any suspicion of malicious intent towards his lineage than to convey his interest in settling the debt. Furthermore, because it is commonly held that a person who has renounced the practice of bad *itonga* will die should he revert to his former behaviour, Mlɔzi's public vow could be used by him to negate any accusation of *-ly-* which might be levelled against him in future. Having taken this vow, Mlɔzi could easily counter any future suggestion of his having consumed someone by the palpable evidence of his continued existence. In short, Mlɔzi acted to nullify the emergent interpretation, which portrayed him as wilfully diminishing his own lineage.

Summary: The Effects of Diagnoses in Terms of Medicines
With the exception of divinations in which a patrilineal kinsman of

the victim is seen as the possessor of the offending medicine, diagnoses of *empongo* in terms of medicine do not lead to attempts to reconcile the disputants. On the whole, these diagnoses remain acted upon only on the symbolic level of the *empongo* itself: people procure counter-medicines and remedies but do not seek redress of underlying differences.

The reason given by informants for this fact is that the medicine makes things equal—that is, the forces involved in the situation become equalized by the counter-medicine. If the victim dies, stronger medicines may be sought to prevent a recurrence in future; if the victim recovers, the remedy has restored the balance.[6]

The parallel between this reciprocal mode of behaviour and the normal transactional mode of interaction between non-kinsmen has been pointed out. We suggest that phrasing the dispute in terms of medicines makes the status relationship, and thus the reciprocal pattern of behaviour, the salient feature of the situation. Since there is no ethical imperative for non-kinsmen to be at peace ('of one heart'), the use of medicines maintains the relationship between the non-kinsmen but with another token substituted for whatever constituted the original basis for the relationship. Stockpiling medicines privately in this way seems to suppress both the underlying conflict and expressions of antagonism sometimes indefinitely or for a considerable length of time (witness the cases of medicinal diagnoses from the diviners' records which had not become public after eight months).

SUMMARY AND CONCLUSIONS

Our analysis has shown that diagnosing a case of *empongo* in terms of medicines initiates a different chain of behaviour, a different set of social processes and dynamics, from that which follows a diagnosis in terms of one of the several manifestations of *itonga*. A diagnosis of medicine typically leads to the covert accumulation of additional medicines. On the other hand, a diagnosis of *itonga* initiates processes which result in either reconciliation or severance of the relationship between the disputants. The contrasting effects of these diagnoses are

[6] This fact explains why some residents of Ipepete came to me for medical assistance only for cases which they attributed to medicines. Since I was a European (i.e. not African) and Europeans obviously have considerable power, they must therefore have powerful medicines. For that reason my remedies were good counters to those prepared by an African.

seen to reflect the different modes of behaviour entailed by the status relationships of non-kinsman and agnate respectively.

Since the aetiological categories of *itonga* and medicine implicitly associate disputes with these categories of relationship (as we demonstrated in the previous chapter), we suggest that it is these terms which condition the subsequent disposal of the disputes. In short, these terms guide the ways in which a dispute is handled by making the status relationship between the disputants the salient aspect of the case, a procedure which then utilizes the norms and values of the status relationship to regulate the outcome.

CHAPTER VI

CONCLUSION

In this final chapter we shall summarize our conclusion about the place of beliefs about *itonga* and medicines in the social life of Mwanabantu tribe and relate them to the question posed by Middleton and Winter which provided the point of departure for the analysis—viz. why do some societies maintain beliefs in both witchcraft and sorcery.

THE PLACE OF BELIEFS ABOUT *ITONGA* AND MEDICINES IN THE SOCIAL LIFE OF MWANABANTU TRIBE

In describing the social structure and organization of Mwanabantu tribe, we showed how relations of incorporation and transaction are expressed in indigenous concepts of descent and non-kinship (including affinity) respectively. We further indicated that all social relations in Mwanabantu may be ordered according to these two fundamental concepts. From this basic understanding of the social situation, we turned to an examination of the aetiology of disease and death, two notions which fuse in the single concept of *empongo* in the Safwa dialect. In this examination we first noted that the health of an individual is believed to be dependent on the state of the incorporative and transactional relationships in which he is involved. Thus *empongo* may be caused by action which shatters (*-nandy-*) incorporative relations or which weakens (*-tul-*) transactional ones.

From this observation we hypothesized that the individual terms used to explain the causes of *empongo* in the indigenous folk aetiology involve disturbances in different kinds of social relationships. We investigated this hypothesis by first compiling the universe of aetiological terms as they arise in the culturally appropriate settings of autopsy and divination (Chapter III) and by then examining how these terms are applied in concrete instances of *empongo* (Chapter IV). We concluded that the application of these various terms does depend on the kind of social relationship between parties engaged in a dispute.

More specifically, disruptions in incorporative relationships of various kinds are symbolized by the operation of the various manifestations of the innate power of *itonga*, while disruption in transactional relations is symbolized by the use of medicines.

We then concluded our analysis by investigating the results of attributing a case of *empongo* to one or another of these aetiological categories. Basically there are two such results. First, with regard to members of the society, these diagnoses seem to serve two purposes. In the first place, since certain kinds of diagnoses concern members of only certain groups, categories of disease aetiology provide an idiom in which group membership may be expressed. Thus, cases of *-ly-* excite the concern of the patrilineage and must not be discussed outside it. On the other hand, cases of *-gun-* galvanize the community, but are of comparatively little interest to outsiders. In the second place, diagnoses of *empongo* enable people to adjust their behaviour to the tensions and power struggles within the society. We have seen that a person's own social position influences which diagnosis of a case he accepts and that he can, by accepting a particular diagnosis, either align himself in an on-going power struggle, as a member of a faction, or opt out of it (as we saw in the development of Cases V and VI). In addition, one can exploit an on-going struggle to further his private concerns, as Ntandala and Wambɛ did in Cases VI and X respectively.

The second result of the differential diagnosis of cases of *empongo* concerns the disposition of the social disruptions which underlie the diagnoses themselves. We observed that disruption in incorporative bonds are handled through symbolic reaffimation of the bond, either at ancestral rites or by an agreed return to 'one heart'; or failing reconciliation, through embarkation on a path of action leading ultimately to severance of the incorporative bond. On the other hand, disruptions in transactional relationships are handled through reciprocal accumulation of medicines. In short, the underlying dispute becomes handled symbolically but in the mode of the relationship itself: with regard to incorporative relationships, by publicly renewing or abjuring commitment to work for the good of the unit; and with regard to transactional relationships, by covertly perpetuating the relationship through the reciprocal activity of stockpiling medicines.

In sum, beliefs about *itonga* and medicines would seem to 'fit into' the Mwanabantu social system (to use Middleton and Winter's phrase) as part of a more inclusive classificatory scheme which regulates social relations. Thus *itonga* and being 'of one heart', on the one hand, and the use of medicines and reciprocal prestations, on the other, constitute two aspects of behaving within the basic incorporative and transactional modes of relationship respectively.

Being 'of one heart' and fulfilling reciprocal obligations (as in the *omwinɛ* relationship, for example) express the positive aspect of these two relationships. That is, they involve adherence to expected behaviour patterns. *Itonga* and medicines, on the other hand, symbolize extraordinary actions within the sphere of the two modes of relationship. *Itonga* involves behaviour which threatens the unity of the incorporative relationship. (Such behaviour, it must be noted, may ultimately be judged to have enhanced rather than destroyed the unity, as when a death is attributed to 'good' rather than 'bad' *itonga*.) Medicines, on the other hand, involve failure to comply with the usual expectations and obligations of a transactional relationship and substitution of extraordinary tokens for customary ones. In short, using *itonga* and using medicines constitute selfish, discordant ways of behaving within the two fundamental modes of association in Mwanabantu society.

The theories of Simmel on the place of conflict in social life relate closely to this Safwa conception. Simmel writes,

Just as the universe needs 'love' and 'hate', that is, attractive and repulsive forces, in order to have any form at all, so society, too, in order to attain a determinate shape, needs some quantitative ratio of harmony and disharmony, of association and competition, of favourable and unfavourable tendencies. But these discords are by no means mere sociological liabilities or negative instances. Definite, actual society does not result only from social forces which are positive, and only to the extent that the negative factors do not hinder them. This common conception is quite superficial: society, as we know it, is the result of both categories of interaction, which thus both manifest themselves as wholly positive (1964:15–16).

This last sociological observation of Simmel finds expression in the Safwa concept of 'good' *itonga*—discordant, perhaps destructive action which is recognized as contributing to the common good.

To return to the question of how the concepts of *itonga* and medicine 'fit into' the social system of Mwanabantu tribe, we are thus suggesting that they provide the idiom for expressing the 'negative' aspect of the fundamental social relationships of incorporation and transaction respectively.

The existence of a 'negative' vocabulary of association paralleling the 'positive' obtains, of course, in our own society as well. For example, two people standing in the status relationship of co-religionist can express their association negatively in accusations of heresy or back-sliding, since these terms convey both discord and association. These terms are quite inappropriate, however, for expressing discord between members of entirely unrelated religious sects. Furthermore, different status relationships have different ways of expressing disharmony while still maintaining the relationship. Thus heresy, while suitable for co-religionists, would be inappropriate to express conflict between parent and child or between employer and employee, for example.

RELEVANCE OF OBSERVATIONS AMONG THE MWANABANTU TO MIDDLETON AND WINTER'S QUESTION

With this point in mind, we now return to the question posed by Middleton and Winter—namely, why do many African societies maintain beliefs in both witchcraft and sorcery. We suggest that these two beliefs constitute a contrast set which may be used in many societies for dichotomizing social relationships of various kinds. We are not suggesting that this ideology is necessarily used in all African societies for differentiating incorporative from transactional relationships, as it is in Mwanabantu society, although Middleton and Winter themselves present some evidence to indicate that this may be so.

These writers observe that in patrilineal societies accusations of witchcraft against women, as opposed to accusations of sorcery, occur only in societies with the house property complex—that is, in societies where property is divided equally among house units in inheritance, where the true levirate is found, and where children are invariably assigned to the social group of the pater rather than the genitor (Gluckman 1950). They cite eight tribes in East and South Africa which support this observation and in which, in addition, almost all accusations are made between co-wives.[1] Then citing Fallers' (1957) observation that a woman is incorporated into her husband's lineage at marriage in societies with the house property complex and not in societies lacking this complex, they conclude,

[1] The eight tribes so cited are: Gusii, Kikuyu, Kamba, Zulu, Swazi, Lovedu, Venda, and Pondo.

Conclusion

A woman in a society with the house property complex, . . . becomes incorporated into her husband's lineage. . . . Since her status in the lineage into which she marries becomes an inalienable part of her social personality, notions of witchcraft conceived as inherent and perverted tendencies of persons in ascribed positions become relevant.

By comparison, in patrilineal societies lacking the house property complex, the wife does not acquire membership in her husband's lineage but instead becomes connected with it by ties which are voluntary and contractual in form. . . . Since the woman's relationship to her husband and his lineage is voluntary and contractual, ideas concerned with perversion of inherent status are not relevant, and such women are accused of practising sorcery rather than witchcraft (Middleton and Winter 1963:16).

Since most accusations of wizardry involving women occur between co-wives, it follows from the above conclusion of Middleton and Winter that when these women are in an incorporative relationship (i.e. both, through marriage, members of their husband's lineage), accusations are phrased in terms of witchcraft; and when they are in a non-incorporative (but not necessarily transactional) relationship (i.e. when they are not absorbed into their husband's lineage), accusations are phrased in terms of sorcery. This evidence thus indicates that the correlation between witchcraft beliefs and incorporative relations, on the one hand, and sorcery beliefs and non-incorporative (transactional?) social relations, on the other, is not simply a phenomenon of Mwanabantu tribe.

Regardless of this evidence, however, we are not necessarily suggesting that this correlation is universally true. In answer to Middleton and Winter's question, we are merely citing Mwanabantu data as illustrative of a general proposition that witchcraft and sorcery beliefs may be utilized in a single society to express conflict within any two contrasted social categories. In Mwanabantu tribe these happen to be between incorporative as opposed to transactional relations; they might be used instead between males as opposed to females or between age sets as opposed to within age sets. On the other hand, social relationships of incorporation and transaction may be symbolized in different terms, as Leach's (1961) comparative observations on five societies suggest.

In sum, our answer to Middleton and Winter's question is that both witchcraft and sorcery beliefs can exist in the same society because they provide categories for symbolizing deviance from the norms of any two social relationships which are in contrast. This conclusion must be tested cross-culturally. At the present time, however, comparative work is hampered by two major flaws in the literature.

First, the terms 'witchcraft' and 'sorcery' have for the most part been employed in a thoroughly chaotic manner. (See Turner [1964] for examples of their inconsistent use even within the single symposium edited by Middleton and Winter.) This situation would appear to be due largely to the fact that investigators have often imposed these analytic categories on the data before examining them first to see what distinctions the people under consideration make themselves. Thus Marwick (1965:81-3), for example, distinguishes witchcraft from sorcery by five criteria *which derive from Zande folk belief*. He then goes on to apply the term 'sorcery' to all beliefs about 'mystical evil-doers' among the Cewa, although some of his own data show that these beliefs share attributes which he claims characterize witchcraft. In Chapter III we have cited other examples of this practice. This terminological morass is a formidable obstruction to comparative work. For one must first uncover the ethnographic reality behind each investigator's terminology, and, in so doing, one often brings unresolvable inconsistencies to light.

These inconsistencies are unresolvable largely because of the paucity of recorded case material, which is the second feature of the literature that presently hampers comparative research on this subject. The generalizations which characterize most ethnographic accounts of witchcraft and sorcery do not provide much data for reanalysis. Only in recent ethnographies employing the extended case study method (e.g. Turner 1957, Middleton 1960) do we find adequate data for further analysis.

In short, the literature itself reflects certain weaknesses in ethnographic method or reporting which presently obstruct comparative work on the problem of the relationship between witchcraft and sorcery, on the one hand, and social categories, on the other. Nevertheless, the effort required to unravel the existing data from various societies (a project beyond the scope of the present inquiry) would undoubtedly be well repaid. In the meantime, collection in the field of detailed case histories should contribute towards a greater understanding of this interesting relationship.

APPENDIX

ADDITIONAL CASE HISTORIES

As indicated in the text, the cases which occurred during the peirod of our field work and were observed in process are marked with asterisks. The proportion of each type of formally diagnosed case will be found in Table VI, Chapter V.

Case XIV[1]*

Incident 1: The Barren Bride. Several months before I entered the field, Danyɛli had consummated a marriage with Sɛlela. From the age of about seven until her marriage at about fifteen, Sɛlela had been raised in the compound of the man her mother had married after she had been divorced by Sɛlela's father. About seven months after Danyɛli and his bride had begun living together, the girl had still not conceived. A diviner was consulted with Sɛlela's mother's brother, Njelwa, acting as go-between. The diagnosis was that people had a medicine which tied Sɛlela's cervix with ropes. Two parties were implicated: first someone standing in the relation of mother to Sɛlela (real or classificatory; *onyina wakwɛ*) was said to be angry because the girl's father had arranged for her bridewealth without any compensation having been given either to her real mother or Njelwa for having raised her;[2] second, Sɛlela's father was said to be angry that Danyɛli's father had still not paid him 200 shillings in outstanding bridewealth. The diviner gave the girl various medicines to ward off harm but cautioned that there must be some rapprochement between the various parties before Sɛlela would conceive.

Several days later Danyɛli's father journeyed to Sɛlela's father's community. According to Danyɛli, an agreeable settlement was reached with him, although the nature of the settlement is unknown to me.

Incident 2: A Premature Birth. Near the close of my stay in the field, about ten months after the above divination, Sɛlela gave birth prematurely, and the infant died after a few hours. Danyɛli reported to me

[1] For comments on this case, see text, pp. 130–1.
[2] In the occasional cases such as this (when a female child lives with her mother's husband past infancy instead of returning to reside with her father, as is customary) a part of the girl's bridewealth is usually given as compensation for having raised the child. The mother is always entitled to a special goat and a sheep out of her daughter's bridewealth.

that when people were drinking beer after the burial, Sɛlela's father had asked if anyone was feeling malice in his heart against the couple. Sɛlela's mother said she was not, but Njelwa admitted that he sometimes felt angry about the disposal of the bridewealth. Danyɛli said that he would talk about this with him, but at the time I left the field a month later, the matter had not been settled.

Case XV*

Mungoni's mother-in-law was stricken with paralysis in her right side and was taken to her brother's, about 15 miles from Ipepete, to stay. A diviner was consulted there, who said that the woman's husband, Jeleshe, had a medicine which was responsible for her illness.

Relations between Jeleshe and his wife's family were not good. I was present when the woman was brought to her brother's, and at the time the brother complained at length that Jeleshe did not treat them properly. He spoke of Jeleshe's failure to send gifts and to allow his wife to visit her kin.

I later learned from informants in Ipepete that Jeleshe married the woman as a widow and had thus paid bridewealth to her first husband's full brothers, as is customary in such a case. However he paid considerably more than the first husband had originally paid (twelve cattle, an exorbitant amount), which made Jeleshe something of a laughing stock in Ipepete. When news of the amount reached the woman's brother, he felt that he should get some of it. Since he had no legitimate claim on the bridewealth, however, he wanted Jeleshe to press the claim. This Jeleshe refused to do, undoubtedly because his wife's first husband was a brother of the Chief and he would have to petition him in his own court for return of part of the bridewealth. Because of Jeleshe's refusal to do this, however, relations with his brother-in-law were strained.

In Ipepete I heard another interesting account of the cause of the woman's illness. This was told me by Sinduda, a woman whose daughter was at one time supposed to marry Mungoni. The marriage had been arranged in Mungoni's and the girl's youth by their fathers. When Mungoni grew up, however, he refused to marry the girl. To express this, he became discourteous towards his intended mother-in-law (the woman whose interpretation of the illness we are here recounting) and also released some of his intended father-in-law's cattle, claiming that they belonged to his own father since he never intended to marry the girl. This behaviour persuaded the girl's parents to abandon all plans of the marriage but left hard feelings between the two families.

This background helps make Sinduda's interpretation of the woman's illness intelligible. She claimed that someone had taken dust from the invalid's footprint and made a medicine to increase their wheat yield.

Since Mungoni was renowned for his wheat fields, there was little doubt whom she was implicating.

Commentary. Both interpretations of the aetiology of the woman's illness point to medicines, although the interpreters were clearly focusing on different disputes. Both disputes, however, involve people of different lineages and different communities.

Case XVI
  Incident 1. Several months before I entered the field, Mayaŋa of Ambobo community had complained to his headman that two members of the headman's classificatory brother's community (Mabandɛ) had made him impotent by means of *itonga*. The headman called a meeting of the elders of the community, at which Mayaŋa failed to appear. This conduct angered the elders, who already knew Mayaŋa as a troublemaker, and nothing further was done about the accusation.
  Incident 2. Mayaŋa suddenly fell sick early in 1964. Reportedly vomiting blood, he consulted a diviner who claimed that his client had been 'speared' (*-las-*). Since this is an affliction only of people engaged in using the power of *itonga* against others, the diviner told Mayaŋa to confess the names of those whom he was attacking. He confessed the names of the two men whom he had previously accused of rendering him impotent.

Commentary. Although this case came to light too late in our field work to discover the underlying cause of the dispute between Mayaŋa and his assailant-victims, it nevertheless indicates that between members of different communities of the same tribe, dissension is expressed in terms of *endasa*.

Case XVII[3]
  The headmen of Igala and Izoko, who were both members of Mwanabantu lineage, were quarrelling over the border between their communities sometime in the late 1940s. An elder of Izoko died, and the cause was diagnosed as *endasa* brought about by the night fighting of the people of *itonga* in the two communities. An informant of mine, who had affines in Igala, recounted that his father-in-law had been 'speared' (*-las-*) in the same nocturnal battles. Although I could not determine the actual number of deaths which were attributed to this battle, people spoke as though the number was considerable.
  Because the headman of Izoko was the British-appointed Chief, the

[3] Comment on this case will be found in Chapter IV, p. 107 and Chapter V, p. 122.

authorities took a particular interest in the case and tried it in Magistrate's court. The Chief (i.e. Izoko) won the case and simultaneously considered himself victor in the nocturnal war as well.

Case XVIII

Hɔswe and his younger brother, Mwanyalɛ did not get along. Hɔswe had two wives, a woman of about forty and another in her early thirties. Neither of these women had conceived in about eight years, although each had several living children. Mwanyalɛ was believed by Hɔswe to have tied their wombs (-*tat*-), a manifestation of *itonga*.

In about 1960 Hɔswe died. His sons consulted a diviner, who said that Mwanyalɛ had consumed (-*ly*-) his brother. Mwanyalɛ was called to and attended a second divination, and at the time of our field work Hɔswe's sons seemed reconciled with their uncle. Indeed, he had even inherited their mother.

The younger of Hɔswe's wives was inherited by a third brother, Mwanande. Although at least a year had elapsed since he had begun having sexual relations with her, she was still not pregnant. Mwanande and his wife's father consulted a diviner, who said that Mwanyalɛ had never removed the ropes with which he had bound her cervix when she was Hɔswe's wife. About six months before we left the field, a meeting was arranged at which Mwanyalɛ reasserted his brotherly feeling towards his lineage and thereby 'unbound' the woman. Although she did not conceive while we were in the field, no overt quarrelling occurred between Mwanyalɛ and Mwanande or the woman's father.

Commentary. The dissension in this case was between agnates and all accusations phrased in terms of manifestations of *itonga*. The fact that the antagonists in the case, Hɔswe and Mwanyalɛ, were brothers and the former's death was attributed to -*ly*- tallies with the social situations and diagnoses in Cases VI and VIII.

This case contrasts well with Case XIV, which also concerned a barren woman. In that case the dispute was between non-agnates of different communities, instead of brothers. Significantly barrenness was attributed to medicines in that case and to a manifestation of *itonga* (-*tat*-) in this one. This contrast corroborates our general conclusion that medicines symbolize disputes between non-kinsmen of different communities and *itonga* symbolizes disagreement among patrilines.

*Case XIX**

In the community of Ntɔndo, a boy, aged about ten, died suddenly, having complained about pains in his stomach the previous day. An autopsy was performed and by the cuts on his liver it was determined

Appendix

that someone had consumed (-*ly-*) him. The operator and headman stated that the culprit was a member of the boy's lineage, who wanted to do something 'big' and so had killed his 'son'.

Further inquiry revealed that two of the lad's classificatory fathers did not get along well. The dissension had reached a point where the 'elder brother' had repeatedly denounced his younger brother's behaviour at ancestor rites. Whether or not a specific issue was at the base of the dissension could not be determined.

Commentary. Although details on this case from another community are rather fragmentary, the correlation between the disputants' social relationship and the diagnosed cause of death supports the conclusion proposed in the text. The implication of the diagnosis was that the 'younger brother' would next attempt to consume the 'older brother'.

Case XX*

Ndɛmbɛla had a trading partner (*omwinɛ*) in Tribe C, to the north of Mwanabantu. In late December 1962, he went to the partner to try to get some sweet potatoes. He stayed about four days and then suddenly fell ill. He remained with his partner several days and then was taken home by members of the partner's family.

A diviner was called who determined the cause of the illness to be a medicine which had been placed in Ndɛmbɛla's food by someone in the community. The diviner spoke of jealousy there over Ndɛmbɛla's closeness with the partner.

Although Ndɛmbɛla died a few days after this divination, nothing further was done.

Commentary. Whether or not jealousy towards Ndɛmbɛla actually existed in his partner's community, we do not know. The significant fact, however, is that it was thought to exist and the aetiology of Ndɛmbɛla's illness was concurrently seen as medicine. Thus we again see the association between the social relationship, non-kinsman of another tribe, and *empongo* diagnosed in terms of medicine.

One of the main reasons why nothing further was done about this death was that Ndɛmbɛla's eldest son was a Christian and refused to consult a diviner again.

Case XXI*

Maligo was a headstrong girl of about fourteen whose father, Kandyandya, had betrothed her to Duwala, a man of about forty. The girl herself had lived in Itimba for a time and was suspected in Ipepete of loose conduct and was notorious for her laziness in cultivating. In addition, her father was known as a rogue who drank too much, was frequently dishonest in his dealings, and tried to seduce other men's wives. Because of the reputations of both father and daughter, many people in Ipepete laughed at Duwula for believing that the marriage had been arranged in good faith.

Maligo became ill and was taken to stay with her mother's kinsmen in a neighbouring tribe. She remained there several weeks, during which time I heard a rumour, which had originated with Kanyandya's half-brother Gazwile, that her father and mother had made a pact to consume (-*ly*-) her in order that her father might become a diviner and witch-doctor.

About two months after Maligo had gone, Kandyandya came to me and asked if I would bring her back to Ipepete. I agreed. Mwashale (Kandyandya's sister's husband), Duwula, and another son-in-law of Kandyandya went with me to fetch the invalid, who was taken to the hut of Kandyandya's mother. The girl really looked very ill, and I offered to stop at the hospital on the return trip. Kandyandya refused, saying that Maligo's was not a sickness that a hospital could cure; '*balodyilɛ*'—that is, foreign substances have been introduced into her body.

This interpretation was based on a divination which Kandyandya had received at his wife's family's. The diviner had indicated that someone in Ipepete bore unexpressed anger towards Kandyandya. This was undoubtedly true, since Kandyandya was not widely trusted because of his ways with women. (One well-known joke about him was that while drunk once, he had even tried to seduce a woman who turned out to be his classificatory sister.) Despite this diagnosis and the attempted remedies, however, Maligo's condition had obviously not improved.

In consequence, a second diviner was summoned when Maligo returned to Ipepete. This diviner said that Maligo had been made ill by a rebuffed suitor from Itimba who had concocted a medicine from her faeces and several plants. The diviner gave the girl counteracting medicines and told Kandyandya to sacrifice to his ancestors.

This divination focused on two other aspects of Kandyandya's and his daughter's social relations. In fact, Maligo had been 'courted' by other men, and this interpretation was therefore plausible. In addition, praying to the ancestors was a way of bringing Kandyandya together in a common activity with his half-brothers Nsyele and Gazwile, with whom he did not get along well. (Witness the rumour started by Gazwile, which is cited above.) A small rite, with just the family attending, was held.

Commentary. This case entailed two formal divinations. The first pointed to Kandyandya's relations with his fellow residents in Ipepete community and diagnosed Maligo's illness as due to -*lody*-; the second referred to Maligo's and her father's relations with an outsider and diagnosed the illness in terms of medicine.

The rumour begun by Gazwile is also significant in phrasing the cause of the girl's illness in terms of -*ly*-, since Gazwile's quarrel was with her patrilineal relative Kandyandya. No further developments occurred with respect to relations between the brothers until the divination following the death of Sinkoshi, reported in Case XXII and, with relevance to this dispute, Case XXIII. Both the formal and the rumoured diagnoses of Maligo's illness thus corroborate the conclusions reached above in the text.

Case XXII[*4]

Zumba was a man of about forty, concerning whom there was considerable controversy in Ipepete. Some claimed that he had good *itonga*, and he often had the headman's ear. On one occasion early in my field work, I was walking past the headman's hut with his son, who was my assistant at the time. We stopped to greet Dendɛ (the headman) and found him whispering with Zumba. My assistant indicated that we should make a hasty departure and later explained that Zumba was 'like' a diviner and was making a report to the headman.

Indeed Zumba consciously cultivated an image of himself as an *omwitonga* by acting rather distant and unapproachable and by letting his hair grow long. Since he was the only person in the community who had long hair, I once asked my assistant about it. He replied that the long hair was to make people 'fear' him.

Zumba was also in favour with Dendɛ for having stood by one of the latter's wives when everyone else left her *ikwila* (co-operative work group). This wife, Mwoga, was bullish and argumentative. Since drinking intensified these qualities, and the outstanding value among *ikwila* members is conviviality at beer parties, people fled her group. Only Zumba remained in her *ikwila* and many considered him a troublemaker for siding with her.

In 1963 at the funeral of Sinkoshi, the oldest woman of the headman's lineage, Zumba publicly accused Mwashale, his sister's husband, of having killed the old lady and of using his *itonga* against the people in the community. As a result of this incident, I questioned informants about relations between Mwashale and Zumba in the past. I learned that they were often at loggerheads and had argued publicly at an *ikwila* beer party at Dendɛ's several years before. The source of their mutual ill will seemed to be their rivalry for a position of prestige; both were vying to be Dendɛ's right hand man.

One day about two months after Sinkoshi's funeral, a friend informed

[4] For comments on this case, see the text, p. 106.

me that Zumba had been ill for some time and asked if I would take him to the hospital. I consented, and ten days later he died there. Although no post-mortem examination was held, the funeral was elaborate and emotion-filled. Several times Zumba's younger brother had to be forcibly restrained from rolling on the ground and tearing his clothes in grief.[5]

Several neighbours were discussing the circumstances of Zumba's death after the funeral and said that Mwashale, Mlɔzi (a reputed *omwitonga* from a neighbouring community; see Case IV) and Kɛya (a resident of the community who had publicly performed certain feats which established him as a man of good *itonga*) had visited Zumba in the hospital. Before the visit the patient had reportedly been recovering well, but soon after he had suffered a relapse and died.

Later I heard this same story from an informant but with several names added to the above three as accomplices to the deed. The accomplices included two sons of Mwashale and two other elders in the community who were considered to have *itonga*. My informant said that these men had joined together to do away with Zumba, using the term *agunɛ* to describe the activity. He also related that one of Mwashale's sons had once gone to Mwoga to offer to work in her *ikwila* again and to bring other workers with him (one of whom he specifically mentioned was Kɛya) if she would oust Zumba. She refused, and the son was said to have replied that they would get Zumba some other way.

Still another informant had approximately the same story, with the additional fact that Zumba had been telling people that Mwashale possessed a medicine which had turned Dendɛ's head and made him believe everything Mwashale said.

Not long after Zumba's death, several of his younger brother's children died as well. Within a month the brother moved to his wife's father's community.[6]

Case XXIII*

Sinkoshi was the oldest surviving woman of Onkoshi lineage and sister of the mother of Nsyele and Gazwile, who were Kandyandya's half-brothers (see Case XXII). En route home from her sister's one evening, she fell into a stream and died. She was discovered late the following morning by her daughter, who went searching for her after learning that she spent the night neither at home nor at her sister's. Although I did

---

[5] Although displays of grief are expected of the deceased's close kinsmen at funerals, this man's behaviour was the most extreme I ever witnessed. Indeed Safwa observers even commented on his state.

Since the father-in-law was a headman in another community, Zumba's brother's move to uxorilocal residence was not unexpected, but the timing quite clearly had something to do with the deaths.

not actually see the body, it was widely reported that she was discovered with her nose and fingernails missing.

At Sinkoshi's funeral Zumba made the accusation against Mwashale reported in Case XXII. Later, however, when Sinkoshi's son, her sister's son Gazwile, and a member of her own lineage consulted a diviner, they learned that she had been killed by an *ombuda* (*ambuda*, plural). *Ambuda* are believed to kill people and use their noses, ears, fingernails, genitals or pubic hair to make medicines to increase the yield from their gardens. The diviner, who lived in Umbwila, claimed that there were three *ambuda* in Ipepete, one woman and two men.

Gazwile and Sinkoshi's son reported the divination to Dendɛ, the Ipepete headman, along with the names of the culprits. Dendɛ was involved in this case both as headman and an elder of Sinkoshi's lineage. No official announcement of the names was ever made, although rumour had it that Kandyandya (Case XXII) and Mwakambɔndya, one of the sons of a co-wife of another sister of Sinkoshi, were the male *ambuda*. The name of the female *ombuda* never came to light. Along with the names which circulated, the rumour also claimed that the diviner would come to pɔint out the *ambuda* and drive them out.

Commentary. This diagnosis, concerning *ambuda*, is anomalous in our data and requires some discussion. We have seen in Case XXII that Kandyandya and his half-brothers did not get along. In the light of our previous observations, one might thus expect this divination, which implicated Kandyandya, to be phrased in terms of *-ly-*, because one of his half-brothers was involved in the seance. We would similarly expect the dissension which existed between Mwakambɔndya and his half-brother to be phrased in terms of *-ly-*. Instead the verdict was that they were *ambuda*. To understand why this diagnosis might have been offered, let us review briefly the history of the concept of the *ombuda*.

The idea of *ambuda* is a recent borrowing by the Safwa from the Wanji, a neighbouring people to the south-east. According to William Garland (personal communication), who studied the Wanji between 1963–5, these people believe in a garden magic made of the soft parts of the body. Those who wish to possess this medicine are said to find a victim out walking at night and then slap his face. Thereafter the victim is said to become very docile and resigned to his fate. He is later told to go to a certain spot at night where he is beaten to death and the body parts removed for the medicine.

In about 1957 a potential victim in Uwanji ran to a European missionary nurse for asylum. The head missionary at the station began an investigation into these practices and went from village to village collecting the names of supposed *ambuda*. He then took these names to the Provincial Commissioner and pressed charges against the *ambuda* himself. Out of the forty or so names which he had collected, slightly less than half were found guilty by a European magistrate in 1957. The culprits were exiled to Ubena, a neighbouring area. According to Garland, there was a resurgence of activity by *ambuda* among the Wanji in 1963, the time the case now under consideration occurred. The diviner who gave the interpretation came from Umbwila, the region of Safwa-Nyiha peoples closest to the Wanji.

Within Ipepete, ideas of how *ambuda* operate differed from Wanji conceptions. According to my informants, the *ombuda* secured his victim's compliance through medicines. Furthermore, his attacks did not necessarily result in the victim's death, since, if the victim was taken to a diviner when the first symptoms (listlessness and speechlessness) of his having been singled out as an *ombuda*'s victim appeared, then medicinal protection against further entrapment could be secured. It would thus seem that this imported category of evil-doing was incorporated into the pre-existing category of medicine by the people of Ipepete.

If this be true, then it would seem to have been applied to a dispute involving people in a social relationship that, from previous observations, we would expect to be associated with -*ly*- not medicines. We suggest, however, that since the disputes which came to light involved sons of sisters of the deceased in conflict with their half-brothers (i.e. brothers by different mothers) that this transactional relationship of membership in different houses overrode the incorporative relationship of membership in the same patrilineage. In short we suggest that because the death which provided the symbol for these two disputes between brothers of different houses was that of the classificatory mother of two of the protagonists, the dispute itself was seen as between houses and therefore as a case caused by medicines.

GLOSSARY

The following is a list of the Safwa terms most frequently used in the text. Nouns are indicated in singular form; to find plural nouns used in the text the reader should consult the following paradigm of plural prefixes.

Singular prefix	Plural prefix
eshi-	evi-
i-	ama-
e-	invariable
on-	ama-
o (nasal)-	a-, ab-

amaya—an affliction which occurs as a complication of a previous illness; believed to be caused by unresolved dissension within the patrilineage.

empaŋa—the men's house of a compound; also the community, whose residents are conceived as residents of the headman's men's house.

empongo—sickness or death; more precisely a weakening or withdrawal of a person's life force.

endasa—an affliction believed to be caused by being speared in a nocturnal battle with a person possessing the power of *itonga*.

enyumba—the 'house', all children of the same woman who have been legitimated by the same bridewealth.

eshiipa—the family estate, consisting of fields and livestock.

eshixɔlɔ—patrilineage. Because political divisions are conceived as the patrilineal territories of the chiefly lineage, we have rendered this word as 'tribe' also.

exaya—the compound, the domestic unit of Safwa society.

ibanza—the men's house of a compound, where sons and male dependants of the compound head reside. The stem with a personal prefix is used to designate the residents of a community who are not members of the headman's patrilineage (cf. *empaŋa*).

igandyɔ—the sacred grove where members of the chiefly lineage are buried.

ikwila—fields worked communally by members of a community under the direction of the headman; corresponds to the headman's family estate.

inzyongoni—life force, power of existence.

itonga—the innate, neutral power to act and not be seen; 'witchcraft'.

Glossary

-las- —spear; may be used to refer to both physical penetration with a sharp pointed object and attack through the power of *itonga* (q.v.).

-lɔdy- —introduce foreign substances (called *amalela*) into another person's body or gardens with malicious intent; accomplished through the power of *itonga* (q.v.).

-ly- —consume a person's vitals through the power of *itonga* (q.v.).

oganga—diagnosis, remedy, oracle.

ogulugulu—procurement of medicine with the specific intent of harming another person; 'sorcery'.

ompena—resident of a compound who is not a member of the compound head's patrilineage; commoner (as opposed to a member of the headman's lineage); orphan; 'stranger-dependent'.

omwɛnɛ—headman.

omwɛnexaya—compound head.

omwitonga—a person possessing the power of *itonga* (q.v.); 'witch'.

omwitɔŋwa—assistant to a headman.

onzimu—ancestor spirit.

onzizi—any substance used to alter a vexing situation; medicine; also specifically infusions prepared from bark or roots.

oŋganga—diagnostician; diviner; medicine man.

ɔmwavi—the bark of a tree or a decoction of this bark, used in former times to test suspected possessors of *itonga*; the ordeal itself.

BIBLIOGRAPHY

Bachmann, Traugott (1943) *Ich gab manchen Anstoss.* Hamburg, Ludwig Appel Verlag.

Barth, Fredrik (1966) *Models of Social Organization.* Royal Anthropological Institute Occasional Paper No. 23. Glasgow, The University Press.

Beidelman, T. O. (1963) 'Witchcraft in Ukaguru', in *Witchcraft and Sorcery in East Africa.* John Middleton and E. H. Winter, eds. London, Routledge & Kegan Paul.

Bohannan, Paul (1957) *Justice and Judgment among the Tiv.* London, Oxford University Press for the International African Institute.

—(1958) 'Extra-processual events in Tiv political institutions', *American Anthropologist* 60.1:1–12.

—(1963) *Social Anthropology.* New York, Holt, Rinehart and Winston.

—(1965) 'The Tiv of Nigeria', in *Peoples of Africa.* James L. Gibbs, Jr., ed. New York, Holt, Rinehart and Winston.

Brock, Beverley (1963) 'A Preliminary Description of the Nyiha People of Southwestern Tanganyika'. Unpublished M.A. thesis, University of Leeds, England.

—(1966) 'The Nyiha of Mbozi', *Tanzania Notes and Records* 65:1–30.

Colson, Elizabeth (1966) 'The alien diviner and local politics among the Tonga of Zambia', in *Political Anthropology.* Marc J. Swartz, Victor Turner, and Arthur Tuden, eds. Chicago, Aldine Publishing Co.

Conklin, Harold C. (1964) 'Ethnogenealogical method', in *Explorations in Cultural Anthropology: Essays Presented to George P. Murdock.* W. H. Goodenough, ed. New York, McGraw Hill.

Cunnison, Ian (1956) 'Perpetual kinship: a political institution of the Luapula peoples', *Human Problems in British Central Africa* 20:28–48.

Douglas, Mary (1963) 'Techniques of sorcery control in Central Africa', in *Witchcraft and Sorcery in East Africa.* John Middleton and E. H. Winter, eds. London, Routledge & Kegan Paul.

—(1967) 'Witch beliefs in Central Africa', *Africa* 37.1:72–80.

East African Statistical Department (1958) *Tanganyika population census, 1957; general African census, August 1957, tribal analysis, Part I.* Nairobi, Government Printer.

Evans-Pritchard, E. E. (1937) *Witchcraft, Oracles and Magic among the Azande.* Oxford, Clarendon Press.

—(1940) *The Nuer.* Oxford, Clarendon Press.

Fallers, L. A. (1957) 'Some determinants of marriage stability in Busoga', *Africa* 27.2:106–23.

Firth, Raymond (1956) *Elements of Social Organization.* London, Watts and Co. (2nd ed.).

Frake, Charles O. (1961) 'The diagnosis of disease among the Subanun of Mindanao', *American Anthropologist* 63.1:113–32.

—(1962) 'The ethnographic study of cognitive systems', in *Anthropology and Human Behaviour.* Thomas Gladwin and William Sturtevant, eds. Washington, The Anthropological Society of Washington.

Fülleborn, Friedrich (1906) *Das deutsche Njassa- und Ruwuma-gebiet, Land und Leute, nebst Bemerkungen über die Schire Länder.* Berlin, Dietrich Reimer.

Gluckman, Max (1950) 'Kinship and marriage among the Lozi of Northern Rhodesia and the Zulu of Natal', in *African Systems of Kinship and Marriage.* A. R. Radcliffe-Brown and D. Forde, eds. London, Oxford University Press.

—(1962) 'African jurisprudence', *Advancement of Science* 18.75:439–54.

—(1963) 'Gossip and scandal', *Current Anthropology* 4.3:307–16.

Goody, Jack (1961) 'The classification of double descent systems', *Current Anthropology* 2.1:3–25.

Gray, Robert F. (1963) 'Some structural aspects of Mbugwe witchcraft', in *Witchcraft and Sorcery in East Africa.* John Middleton and E. H. Winter, eds. London, Routledge & Kegan Paul.

Gulliver, Philip H. (1955) *The Family Herds: a Study of Two Pastoral Tribes of East Africa, the Jie and Turkana.* London, Routledge & Kegan Paul.

Harwood, Alan (1964) 'Beer drinking and famine in a Safwa village: a case of adaptation in a time of crisis', *Proceedings of the East African Institute of Social Research Conference.* January 1964.

Huntingford, G. W. B. (1963) 'Nandi witchcraft', in *Witchcraft and Sorcery in East Africa.* John Middleton and E. H. Winter, eds. London, Routledge & Kegan Paul.

Kamarck, Andrew Martin (1965) 'Economics and economic development', in *The African World.* Robert A. Lystad, ed. New York, Praegar.

Kootz-Kretschmer, Elise (1926–9) *Die Safwa: ein ostafrikanischer Volksstamm in seinem Leben und Denken.* Berlin, Dietrich Reimer Verlag.

Krige, J. D. (1947) 'The social function of witchcraft', *Theoria* 1:8–21.

Leach, E. R. (1961) *Rethinking Anthropology.* London School of Economics Monographs on Social Anthropology, No. 22. London, Athlone Press.

Marwick, M. G. (1952) 'The social context of Cewa witch beliefs', *Africa* 22.2:120–35; 22.3:215–33.

—(1963) 'The sociology of sorcery in a central African tribe', *African Studies* 22.1:1–21.

Bibliography

—(1965) *Sorcery in its Social Setting: a Study of the Northern Rhodesian Cewa*. Manchester, Manchester University Press.

McCulloch, J. S. G. (1962) 'Measurements of rainfall and evaporation', *East African Agricultural and Forestry Journal* 27, special issue: 115–17.

McLennan, J. F. (1896) 'Some examples of fabricated genealogies adduced to show the readiness of men in all times to fabricate genealogies', in *Studies in Ancient History*. Eleanora A. McLennan and Arthur Platt (eds.). London.

Mead, George Herbert (1964) *On Social Psychology*: Selected papers edited by Anselm Strauss. Chicago, University of Chicago Press. (Phoenix edition.)

Middleton, John (1960) *Lugbara Religion: Ritual and Authority among an East African People*. London, Oxford University Press for the International African Institute.

—(1963) 'Witchcraft and sorcery in Lugbara', in *Witchcraft and Sorcery in East Africa*. John Middleton and E. H. Winter, eds. London, Routledge & Kegan Paul.

Middleton, John and E. H. Winter (1963) *Witchcraft and Sorcery in East Africa*. London, Routledge & Kegan Paul.

Moffett, J. P. (ed.) (1958) *Handbook of Tanganyika*. Dar es Salaam, Government Printer.

Morris, Charles (1955) *Signs, Language, and Behaviour*. New York, George Braziller, Inc. (Reprint of 1946 edition.)

Nadel, S. F. (1952) 'Witchcraft in four African societies: an essay in comparison', *American Anthropologist* 54:18–29.

—(1954) *Nupe Religion*. New York, Free Press of Glencoe.

Needham, Rodney (1966) 'Age, category, and descent', *Bijdragen tot de Taal-, Land-en Volkenkunde* 8:1–35.

Price-Williams, D. R. (1962) 'A case study of ideas concerning disease among the Tiv', *Africa* 32.2:123–31.

Sahlins, Marshall (1961) 'The segmentary lineage: an organization of predatory expansion', *American Anthropologist* 63.2:322–45.

Simmel, George (1964) *Conflict and the Web of Group Affiliations*. Translated from the German by Kurt H. Wolff and Reinhard Bendix. New York, Free Press of Glencoe (paperback edition).

Sturtevant, William C. (1964) 'Studies in ethnoscience', *American Anthropologist* 66.3.2:99–131.

Tempels, Placide (1959) *Bantu Philosophy*. Translated by C. King. Paris, Présence Africaine.

Thomson, Joseph (1881) *To the Central African Lakes and Back*. Boston, Houghton, Mifflin & Co.

Turner, Victor W. (1957) *Schism and Continuity in an African Society: a*

Study of Ndembu Village Life. Manchester University Press for the Rhodes-Livingstone Institute.

—(1964) 'Witchcraft and sorcery: taxonomy versus dynamics', *Africa* 34.4:314–25.

Wilson, Godfrey (1936) 'An African morality', *Africa* 9.1:75–99.

Wilson, Monica (1951) 'Witch beliefs and social structure', *American Journal of Sociology* 56:307–13.

—(1958) *The Peoples of the Nyasa-Tanganyika Corridor.* Communications from the School of African Studies, University of Cape Town ns., 29. Cape Town.

—(1963) *Good Company: a Study of Nyakyusa Age Villages.* Boston, Beacon Press (paperback edition).

Winter, E. H. (1956) *Bwamba: a Structural-functional Analysis of a Patrilineal Society.* Cambridge, Heffer.

Unpublished Material

Court Records, Ilomba Local Court, Mbeya Area, Tanzania.

Mbeya District Book. Mbeya Area Office, Mbeya, Tanzania.

Southern Highlands Provincial Book. Southern Highlands Region Office, Mbeya, Tanzania.

INDEX

Abibanza (the general public), 12, 14, 34
Abine, see Trading partners
Abitonga (sing., *omwitonga*), df. 152; *see Itonga,* Witchcraft
Agriculture: agricultural cycle, 50; cash crops, 7; crops, 5; division of labour, 5–6; organisation of fields, 16–17
Aholo (kinsmen), 34
Akuba (clairvoyants), 45, 46
Alagule, see Divination
Amaya ('complications'), df. 151; 68, 79–80, 108–9, 116
Ambuda, 149–50
Ancestors: categories, 34; control of weather by, 17; infliction of *empongo* by, 55–7, 79, 116–17; protection of descendants, 9, 17, 30, 44–6, 79, 97
Ancestral rites, Plates II, III, and IV; occasions for, 17, 22, 26, 32, 33, 37–8, 116–17; procedures, 32–7, 93, 95
Apena (sing., *ompena*), df. 152; *see* Stranger-dependants
Asians, 6, 7
Autopsies: ban on, 54–5, 80, 106–7; diagnosis by, 60–1, 67, 68, 84, 110, 114–15; incidence of, 16, 54–5, 106–7
Avoidances, 28
Azande tribe, 69–71, 140

Bachmann, Traugott, 1 fn. 1
Barrenness and Infertility, 50, 51, 61, 112 Table VI, 131, 141, 144
Barth, Fredrik, 9
Beer-drinking: at ancestral rites, 17, 18, 32, 35–6, 37, 102; at birth ceremony, 28; by co-operative work groups, 6, 147; during marriage contract, 27, 28
Beidelman, T. O., 72
Birth, *see* Childbirth
Borrowing of new concepts: Supreme Being, 34–5; *ambuda,* 149–50
Brock, Beverley, 1 fn. 1, 2
Bohannan, Paul, xvii fn. 6, 74

Bride-service, 27
Bridewealth, 16, 67 fn. 4; acquisition of, 8, 19, 24; disputes over, 15, 84, 97, 123, 141, 142; means of payment, 6; return of, 97, 105; rights to, 23–4
Brothers, relations between, 16, 19, 23–25, 33, 80–1, 94–5, 98, 116, 119, 144, 145, 148–50
Bungu tribe, 5, 8, 93, 95

Cash, circulation of, 8; *see also* Agriculture, Exchange, Wage Labour
Categories, folk and analytic, xvii, 69–76; social, *see* Social Structure
Cewa tribe, 140
Chiefs, 78–9, 93–4, 122, 143–4; chiefly lineage, 119–20
Childbirth, 28, 30
Christianity, 34, 35 fn. 2
Clairvoyants, *see Akuba*
Colson, Elizabeth, 111 fn. 2
Commensality, 16, 17, 27–8, 36–7, 41, 67
Community (*empaŋa*), df. 151; 10, 13–19; as headman's compound, 14–15; relations between communities, 87–8, 105, 106, 113, 121–2, 143–4; use of medicines by, 63
Community headmen, 14, 15–17, 93–6, 143–4
Compound, 9, 10–13, 11 Fig. 1, 14, 63; authority within, 16
Compound head, 10, 12–13, 14, 16
Conception, 30, 97
Conklin, Harold C., x, 79
Copperbelt, Zambian, 7–8
Cunnison, Ian, 29 fn. 13

Death, 31, 38, 56–8; *see also* Empongo
Debts, 24–5, 64, 67–8, 91–2, 131–2; of hospitality, 88
Descent, *see* Incorporation, Patrilineage
Deviant behaviour, 30, 37–44, 46, 129
Disease, xvi–xvii, 31–2, 49–50, 57–8; *see also* Empongo

Disputes, and the aetiology of *empongo*, xvii, 46–7, 99, 107–9; boundary, *see* Land, boundary disputes; resolution of, 115–18, 121–2, 125–7, 130–2, 133–4; *see also* Judicial procedures

Divination: diagnoses, 81, 85–6, 91–2, 94, 110–16, 112 Table VI, 146; diviners, 44–5, 48–9; fees, 52; frequency of consultation, 51 Table 1; outcomes of, 111–12, 120–7, 132–4; situations requiring, 12–13, 46, 49–51, 51 Table 1; techniques, 52–4

Domestic cycle, 10, 19–20, 25

Douglas, Mary, xv fn. 3, 77

Dreams, 45

Ecology, ix, 2, 5

Economy, *see* Agriculture, Exchange, Hunting, Land, Wage Labour

Empaŋa ('community'), df. 151; *see* Community

Empongo ('disease and death'), df. 151; xvi fn. 5, 30–1; and social control, 37–8, 43–7, 133–7; causes of, 49–50, 55–66, 77, 82, 87, 101–2; *see* Chapters IV and V, *passim*

Endasa, df. 151; 68, 84–9, 106–7, 121–4, 143

Enyumba, df. 151; *see also* 'House'

Epidemics, 95–7, 118, 120

Eshiipa (family estate), df. 151; 6, 10, 12, 15, 19, 80, 93, 116

Eshixɔlɔ, df. 151; 9, 19–20; *see also* Patrilineage, Tribe

Evans-Pritchard, E. E., xv fn. 2, xvi, fn. 4, 69, 70, 75, 77

Exaya, df. 151; *see* Compound

Exchange, 6–8, 26–9

Fallers, Lloyd A., 138

Family estate, *see Eshiipa*

Firearms, 7

Firth, Raymond, 9

Frake, Charles, xvii

Fülleborn, Friedrich, 1

Funerals, 16, 32, 33, 57, 93, 148

Garland, William, 149, 150

Genealogies: alterations in, 23, 93–94, 96, 119–20; shallowness of, 20, 38–9

Gluckman, Max, 16 fn. 10, 110, 138

God, *see* Supreme Being

Goody, Jack, 20

Gray, Robert F., 74

Gulliver, Philip H., 20 fn. 11

Gusii tribe, 138 fn. 1

Harvest ceremony, 32

Headmen, *see* Community Headmen

'House', df. 151; 9–10, 23–6, 117, 149–150

Hunting, 6–7

Huntingford, G. W. B., 74

Hyena-men, 61, 62

Ikwila (community fields), df. 151; 14–15, 16–20, 93, 147

Impotence, 143

Incorporation, relations of, 9–26, 63–4, 65, 109, 126–7, 135–7; and medicines, 63–5

Inheritance, 12, 16, 18, 19, 23, 25, 83, 116

Ipepete: location, 2; population, 2

Inzyongoni ('life force'), df. 151; 30–1, 42–3, 47, 56, 60, 66, 68

Itonga ('witchcraft'), df. 151; xvii, 48–9, 57–62, 69–75; and medicines, 66, 110; as cause of *empongo*, 57–62; bad *itonga*, 58–61, 92, 102, 109, 113, 120, 131–2; good *itonga*, 58–61, 92, 120, 124, 137, 147; public displays of, 59–60; relation between victim and culprit, 92, 98; cf. other African concepts of witchcraft, 69–74; *see also* Witchcraft

Judicial procedures, 12–13, 15–16, 18, 19, 22, 60, 81–2, 121–5

Jumbes (lowest official in local government administration), 78, 84, 85, 86, 87, 94; jumbeship, 95

Kaguru tribe, 72

Kamarck, Andrew, 8 fn. 6

Kamba tribe, 138 fn. 1

Kikuyu tribe, 138 fn. 1

Kootz-Kretschmer, Elise, 1, 23, 35 fn. 2, 53

Krige, J. D., 78

Labour, division of, 5–7, 12, 15–18, 23; for wages, *see* Wage Labour; migration, 7–8

Land: acquisition of, 10, 18, 19, 23, 27, 102; availability of, 20; boundary

Index

disputes, 60, 87–8, 102, 107, 122, 143; custodian of, 18
Leach, E. R., 9, 139
'Leagues' (*echama*), 59, 61–2, 85
'Life force', see *Inzyongoni*
Lineage, see Patrilineage
Livestock, 6, 10, 12, 68; see also Bridewealth
Local Executive Officer, 79, 80
Lovedu tribe, 138 fn. 1
Lugbara tribe, 72–3

Magic, the concept of, 75, 130; see also Medicines
Magistrates, 79
Malila tribe, 1
Marriage, 24, 26–8; see also Bridewealth
Marwick, M. G., 78, 140
Mbugwe tribe, 74
Mbwila tribe, 1
McLennan, J. F., 20 fn. 11
Mead, George Herbert, 47
Medical specialists, 48–9; medicine men, 66–8
Medicines, 62–8; and *itonga*, 66, 109, 110–13; and magic, 75–6; and 'vital force', 65–6, 68, 127–8, 129; as cause of *empongo*, 62–8, 127ff; counter-medicines, 129, 133; frequency of this diagnosis, 113; good and bad medicines, 75–6; kinds of, 62–8
Methods, ethnographic, ix–x, 37, 42, 50, 55, 62 fn. 3, 72 fn. 7, 77–8, 111, 140
Middleton, John, xv, 71, 72–3, 78, 136, 138, 139
Mines, x, 8
Morris, Charles, 110
Murder, 67, 108
Mwanabantu tribe, xvi, fn. 4; legends, 14, 18; segmentary organisation, 22; structural features, 29; territory, 13–14

Nadel, S. F., 78
Naming, 28
Nandi tribe, 74
Needham, Rodney, 20 fn. 11
Ngoni tribe, 93
Nyakyusa tribe, 1 fn. 1, 59 fn. 2, 69
Nyiha peoples, 1, 2, 5

Ogulugulu ('sorcery'), df. 152; see Medicines

Omwɛnɛ, see Community Headmen
Omwitɔŋwa (assistant headman), df. 152; 18
Ongolobe, see Supreme Being
Onzizi, df. 152; 62, 63 Fig. 4; see also Medicines
Ordeals, 114–15, 117, 118
Owl-men, 61, 62

Patrilineage, 9, 19–20, 22; corporate responsibilities of, 9, 19–20, 28, 65, 67, 68; disputes within, 68, 99, 105, 106, 109, 113–16, 120–1; lineage fission, 98, 117–18, 120; lineage fusion, 93–4, 96, 119–20; patrilineal ethic, 9, 114, 116, 120, 121, 126; relations between, 93, 96, 102; segmentary nature of, 22–3, 21 Fig. 2
'Poisoning', 65
Political organization, 1, 15–17, 20–3; political change, 78–9, 93–4, 106, 114–15; see also Chiefs, Community Headmen
Pondo tribe, 138 fn. 1
Population, 1, 15 fn. 9
Price-Williams, D. R., 74

Rainfall, 5; ancestors' control of, 17, 119
Ritual, for harvest, Plate I; marriage, 27–8; funerary, 32, 54–5, 57, 80, 148; to end blood feud, 67; to terminate special states (*enboyɔ*), 64; see also Ancestral rites

Sacred groves (sing., *igandyɔ*), df. 151; 32, 95
Sacrifice, 33, 35–6, 67, 119; distribution of sacrificial animals, 33, 35, 36
Safwa language, x, 33–4, 151; linguistic classification, 1
Sahlins, Marshall, 22
Seance, see Divination
Settlement pattern, Plate Ia, 21 Fig. 2, 13
Simmel, Georg, 137
Slater, Mariam, 1 fn. 1
Social structure, 9–29, 135–7; and symbolism of disputes, 65, 99, 105–109, 113, 125–7, 132–7; relations of incorporation, 9–26, 63–4, 135–7; relations of transaction, 26–9, 135–7
Sorcery, df. xv; xvi–xvii, 75, 138–40; see Medicines

Stranger-dependants, 12, 14, 15 fn. 9, 18
Supreme Being, 17, 34–5, 55
Sturtevant, William C., xvii, 79
Sangu tribe, 1 fn. 1, 2, 5, 8
Swazi tribe, 138 fn. 1
Swidden cultivation, 5
Symptoms and diagnoses, relation between, 56–7, 59, 60–1, 67, 68, 82–3, 88–9

Tanganyika: independence, 78–9
Taxation, 6, 8
Tempels, Placide, 31 fn. 1
Temperature, 5
Theft, 50–2, 64, 103
Thomson, Joseph, 1
Tiv tribe, 74
Tonga tribe, 111 fn. 2
Trading partners, 26, 145
Transaction, relations of, 26–9, 109, 127, 132–3, 135–7; use of intermediaries in, 27, 51–2
Tribe, df. xvi fn. 4; 1, 9, 22–3, 28–9, 64; map of Safwa, 4

Turner, V. W., 78, 140

Venda tribe, 138 fn. 1
Village Development Committee, 85

Wage Labour, 7–8, 12, 24, 80, 83, 119 fn. 3
Wanji tribe, 149–50
Warfare, 22–3; by means of *itonga*, 60, 122, 143–4
White Place, the (realm of the ancestor spirits), 31, 33, 56
Wilson, Godfrey, 59 fn. 2
Wilson, Monica, 1, 59 fn. 2, 78
Winter, Edward H., xv, xvi, 20 fn. 11, 71, 136, 138, 139
Witchcraft, df. xv–xvi; moral neutrality of, 59, 69–75, 88, 138–40; *see also itonga*
Wizardry, df. xv; *see also* Witchcraft, Sorcery

Zulu tribe, 138 fn. 1